Northern Ireland Travel Guide

2024-2025

The Complete travel companion and tourist guide to help you explore The Northern Ireland like a Pro, Plus A 5-Day Itinerary in the Cities

Kerri J. Fisher

Copyright © 2024 by Kerri J. Fisher.

All rights reserved.

No part of this book may be reproduced or transmitted in any form or by any means, electronic or mechanical, including photocopying, recording, or by any information storage and retrieval system, without permission in writing from the publisher.

The information in this book is for educational purposes only. The author and publisher are not liable for any damages or losses that may occur as a result of the use of this information.

The author and publisher make no representations or warranties with respect to the accuracy or completeness of the contents of this book and specifically disclaim any implied warranties of merchantability or fitness for a particular purpose.

Table Of Content

Table Of Content _____ 2
Introduction _____ 6
Chapter 1 _____ 10
   A Brief Overview of Northern Ireland _____ 10
      The History of Northern Ireland _____ 13
      Reasons to Visit Northern Ireland _____ 17
      Map of Northern Ireland _____ 20
Chapter 2 _____ 22
   The Best Time To Visit _____ 22
      Northern Ireland in the Spring _____ 23
      Northern Ireland in the summer _____ 24
      Northern Ireland in Autumn _____ 24
      Northern Ireland in the winter _____ 25
   Travel Tips to Know Before Visiting _____ 26
   How To Get To Northern Ireland _____ 35
      How to Get to Northern Ireland By Air _____ 35
      How to get to Northern Ireland from the Republic by Car, Bus, or Train _____ 38
      How to get to Northern Ireland by Sea _____ 40
   Visa requirements and customs regulations _____ 42
      Visa Requirements: _____ 42
      Customs Regulations: _____ 43

Chapter 3 — 46

Accommodation options in Northern Ireland — 46

- Estimated Fees for Accommodation — 46
- Accommodation in Belfast — 46
- Accommodation on the Causeway Coast and Glens — 48
- Accommodation in Derry Londonderry — 49
- Accommodation in Fermanagh Lakelands — 52
- South Down Accommodation - St. Patrick's Country and the Mournes — 53
- Northern Ireland has 10 beautiful places to stay. — 54

Getting Around Northern Ireland — 65

Northern Ireland Packing Essentials — 69

- What Women Should Pack — 73
- What Women Should Wear in Ireland in the Winter — 76
- What Men Should Wear in Ireland — 78
- What Men Should Wear in Winter — 79

Chapter 4 — 86

Northern Ireland's Best Beaches and Islands — 86
Best Things To Do — 97
Top Museums — 121

Chapter 5 — 128

Food and Drink in Northern Ireland — 128

- Northern Ireland Food — 128

Shopping in Northern Ireland — 136

- Chapter 6 146
  - 5 days Northern Ireland Itinerary 146
    - DAY 1 146
      - Morning. 146
      - Afternoon. 146
      - Evening. 147
    - DAY 2 147
      - Morning. 147
      - Afternoon. 147
      - Evening. 148
    - DAY 3 148
      - Morning. 148
      - Afternoon. 148
      - Evening. 149
    - DAY 4 149
      - Morning. 149
      - Afternoon. 149
      - Evening. 150
    - DAY 5 150
      - Morning. 150
      - Afternoon. 150
      - Evening. 151
- Conclusion 152
- Reference 154

Explore norther Ireland with
Confident

Introduction

Welcome to Northern Ireland, a magical place full of beautiful scenery, fascinating history, and welcoming people.

As you set out on your adventure to this lovely location, you might run into the same problem that a lot of travelers do: getting around without a trustworthy friend to help you discover the hidden jewels and cultural quirks.

Based on statistical data, a considerable proportion of tourists have reported that the trip was confusing, with them failing to fully appreciate Northern Ireland because of the lack of direction.

Don't worry—this travel guide will serve as your pass to an easy and rewarding journey.

Without the assistance of a well-written travel guide, navigating the complex landscape of Northern Ireland may be an intimidating undertaking.

From the fabled Giant's Causeway to Belfast's energetic city life, the region's many attractions necessitate more than a cursory glance.

Even the most experienced visitor may become confused by regional traditions, accents, and lesser-known locations.

Imagine yourself at a fork in the road, uncertain about which way to go, at the intersection of historical stories, natural wonders, and traditional taverns.

It's during these times that the lack of a trustworthy friend becomes painfully obvious.

Traveler, do not be alarmed; this guide will help you discover the mysteries of Northern Ireland.

You'll find hidden gems that the uninitiated eye misses, as well as the must-see landmarks as you turn through its pages.

Our guide is made to be with you at every turn, whether your goal is to experience the hustle and bustle of the city streets or the peace and quiet of the Mourne Mountains.

Just picture how much easier it would be to have a reliable guide who could tell you the history of old castles, suggest quaint restaurants nearby, and provide you insight into the subtle cultural differences that make Northern Ireland so distinctive.

Traveling without a carefully chosen guide is like sailing a ship without a compass.

It's an invitation to ambiguity, to pass up chances, and, above all, to the real experiences that are what really make travel unforgettable.

The thrill of discovery can sometimes be overshadowed by the frustration of lost and uncharted territory.

But when you pick up this guide, you're getting more than just a book—you're getting a trustworthy friend who wants to make your journey even better.

Let this book serve as your lighthouse when traveling in Northern Ireland. Allow it to serve as a link between you and this fascinating place's intricate design.

With its perceptive suggestions, insider information, and useful counsel, our guide is your go-to resource for avoiding any potential hazards when traveling in Northern Ireland on your own.

Thus, as you get ready for your vacation, keep in mind that having this friend at your side will mean that every move you make will be informed by experience, making your trip to Northern Ireland an unforgettable experience rather than just travel. Embark on an enlightening voyage where each page becomes a remarkable section of your personal Northern Irish narrative.

Chapter 1

A Brief Overview of Northern Ireland

Northern Ireland is the United Kingdom's smallest nation. It is a part of the United Kingdom, along with England, Scotland, and Wales, yet it is located on the island of Ireland in Western Europe.

Northern Ireland accounts for one-sixth of Ireland, while the remainder of the country is an autonomous republic known as the Republic of Ireland.

Despite its limited geographical size, Northern Ireland is a culturally rich region that has produced notable authors such as Seamus Heaney and C.S. Lewis, as well as notable performers such as Liam Neeson, James Nesbitt, and Kenneth Branagh.

Top ten facts

1. Although Northern Ireland is a part of the United Kingdom, it has its own set of laws. Stormont refers to the Northern Ireland government's Parliament buildings in Belfast.

2. Northern Ireland is the UK's second most thinly populated country, behind Scotland.

3. The island of Ireland was split into two halves in 1921. Northern Ireland remained a part of the United Kingdom, while the remainder of Ireland became known as the Republic of Ireland.

4. Despite the fact that English is the most frequently spoken language in Northern Ireland, Chinese is the most widely spoken minority language!

5. There are six counties in Northern Ireland: Antrim, Armagh, Derry (Londonderry), Tyrone, Fermanagh, and Down.

6. Lough Neagh is a massive lake in Northern Ireland; in fact, it is the largest lake in the British Isles, with every county save Fermanagh touching the lake's shoreline!

7. The Giant's Causeway is a well-known rocky stretch of shoreline in County Antrim. It was produced by previous volcanic eruptions and is made up of hundreds of hexagonal chunks of granite.

8. Belfast is Northern Ireland's capital city. Belfast has been a part of the land since the Bronze Age!

9. Northern Ireland has a population of around 1.8 million people.

10. Ulster is another name for Northern Ireland. Ulster is a nine-county Irish province, six of which are part of Northern Ireland.

Did you know that?

Belfast has 157 wet days on average every year, which is fewer than Scotland, but the capital of Northern Ireland is still wetter than Dublin, the Irish capital!

The Titanic, the world's most renowned ship, was constructed and launched from Belfast Harbour. It was the biggest man-made moving object on Earth when it launched! The Titanic was constructed in 1911 by the Belfast shipyard Harland & Wolff. On April 15, 1912, the RMS Titanic sank after colliding with an iceberg on her maiden voyage.

Although Northern Ireland is commonly referred to as Ulster, the historical Ulster-covered regions are now in the Republic of Ireland.

Northern Ireland obviously attracts young people! Almost 46% of Northern Ireland's entire population is under the age of 30.

There are no snakes or toads in the country, as there are in the rest of Ireland!

Northern Ireland is barely 13 miles from the Scottish shore at its closest point. On a clear day, it is said that you may stand in Antrim and gaze over the ocean to see buildings in Scotland!

Northern Ireland has qualified for three World Cups, in 1958, 1982, and 1986, and George Best is widely regarded as one of the country's most renowned players. Snooker player Alex Higgins and Formula One driver Eddie Irvine are two more Northern Ireland sporting superstars.

The History of Northern Ireland

Northern Ireland's history is a bit confusing! The Kings of England took control of Ireland over 800 years ago, but the Irish eventually drove the English out! However, in the mid-1600s, the legendary English military commander Oliver Cromwell seized control of all of Ireland. Because England was Protestant and Ireland was Catholic, there was a lot of animosity between the two countries.

By the nineteenth century, many individuals in Northern Ireland were Protestants with English ancestors. And here is where troubles developed since the majority of Northern Irish people did not desire independence like the rest of Ireland.

People who wished for an independent Ireland were known as republicans or nationalists because they desired Ireland to become a republic, a government in which people meet to determine laws.

People who opposed Irish independence were referred to as unionists because they wanted to maintain Ireland's union with the United Kingdom. The majority of unionists resided in Northern Ireland.

By 1921, the United Kingdom had decided to recognize Ireland as an independent country, although Northern Ireland was still subject to the Government of Ireland Act.

Unfortunately, this did not put an end to the troubles. Why is this so? Republicans were prepared to fight to keep Northern Ireland separate from the rest of Ireland, while Irish unionists were willing to fight to keep it separate. There were several demonstrations and rioting.

When British soldiers were ordered to avoid religious bloodshed between Protestants and Catholics in 1969, the crisis erupted. The conflicts between the two factions were dubbed the Troubles.

One of the most prominent episodes of the Troubles was Bloody Sunday. It happened on January 30, 1972, when British forces shot 28 civilians, killing 14.

The Belfast Agreement, often known as the Good Friday Agreement since it was signed on April 10, 1998, was a watershed moment. It was an agreement between the British and Irish governments, as well as the majority of Northern Ireland's political parties, on how Northern Ireland should be administered.

The Northern Ireland National Assembly was founded in 1998 as a result of a referendum in Northern Ireland. The UK government has delegated significant responsibilities to the Northern Ireland Assembly. This implies that instead of MPs (Members of Parliament) in London, local politicians now make critical choices on how Northern Ireland is governed.

Many tensions in Northern Ireland have been caused by religion. The majority of Irish people are Christians, although in Northern Ireland, the Protestant Church predominates, whilst the Roman Catholic Church predominates in the neighboring Republic of Ireland. This has produced numerous conflicts between Ireland's two faiths, but things are improving.

Despite being the patron saint of Ireland, St. Patrick was born in Britain, not Ireland! Some speculate that he was abducted as a youngster and taken to Ireland. St. Patrick is credited with introducing Christianity to Ireland. St. Patrick's Day is observed yearly in Northern Ireland on March 17, as it is in the rest of Ireland. It is a public holiday, and festivities often include public parades and festivals, as well as the wearing of green clothing or shamrocks.

Agriculture is one of Northern Ireland's most significant sectors, with over 29,000 farmers actively operating.

Belfast is the most populous city in Northern Ireland, with more than a third of the population residing in or around the capital. Londonderry, sometimes known as Derry, is the second biggest city in Northern Ireland after Belfast. It is located in the northwest of the nation, beside the Foyle River.

The pound sterling is the currency of the nation, as it is in the rest of the United Kingdom.

Although English is the most widely spoken language, Irish (or 'Irish Gaelic') and Ulster Scots are also important. Other languages, such as Chinese, Urdu, and Polish, are becoming increasingly widespread as more individuals from other countries move to Northern Ireland.

The 'Ulster Fry' is one of Northern Ireland's most popular meals: bacon, egg, soda bread, sausage, potato bread, mushrooms, fried tomato, and baked beans! Potatoes are an essential component of Northern Irish cuisine. Champ (mashed potato with spring onions), farl (potato bread), and boxty (potato cake) are traditional foods.

Northern Ireland loves sports! Football, Gaelic football, and rugby union are the most popular, although athletics, boxing, cricket, golf, hurling (an outdoor stick-and-ball game akin to hockey and lacrosse that is traditional in Ireland), and snooker are also popular.

Reasons to Visit Northern Ireland

Northern Ireland's strong qualities include history, natural beauty, magnificent seafood, and Hollywood prestige. Here are 5 reasons why you should place a trip to the North at the top of your bucket list...

1 - It is home to the magnificent Titanic Belfast.

Being named the "World's Leading Tourist Attraction" is no small task, but Titanic Belfast did just that at the 2016 World Travel Awards. Titanic Belfast is a genuine 'wow' experience, standing magnificently at the top of the slipway where the Titanic was constructed. The size of the edifice corresponds to the magnitude of the ill-fated ship.

Inside, multimedia exhibits trace the Titanic's history, development, and demise, while outdoors, the perfect attention to detail, such as the Titanic Memorial Garden, takes your breath away. The garden, which is located on the Olympic slipway, is made up of four grass lawns alternating with wood decking, with proportions indicating the number of Titanic casualties and survivors from each passenger class and crew.

2 - The Causeway Coast is much more stunning in person.

Crashing waves, volcanic vistas, and seals bobbing in the surf... no, this isn't an episode of 'Blue Planet,' but simply another day on the gorgeous Causeway Coast. The Causeway Coast, dubbed one of the 'world's finest road excursions,' winds across Ireland's North-East coast, beginning in Belfast and meandering through the nine glens of Antrim before concluding in the Walled City of Derry.

The Causeway Coast's greatest beauty is, of course, the Giant's Causeway, a UNESCO World Heritage site. According to legend, this huge stretch of approximately 40,000 interlocking hexagonal stone columns was built by local giant Finn McCool. The truth (lava cooling 60 million years ago) is rather different, but the fact remains that the Giant's Causeway is one of Northern Ireland's most valuable assets, and for good cause.

3 - Belfast will astound you.

Since the signing of the Good Friday Agreement in 1998, Belfast has gone a long way. Belfast has evolved as a cosmopolitan, friendly, and inviting city with so much to offer over 25 years after The Troubles and after strong investment. The city hums with a combination of history and redevelopment, from the energy of St George's Market to the ultra-modern Titanic area to the fashionable Commercial Court or old City Hall.

4 - The cuisine is fantastic.

With over 75% of Northern Ireland's countryside dedicated to agriculture, it's no wonder that the cuisine in this part of the globe adheres to a real 'farm to fork' ethic. After all, chefs don't have to go far to get fresh food! Belfast is unquestionably the foodie capital of Northern Ireland, with three restaurants keeping their Michelin star status until 2021 (Ox Belfast, Deanes Eipic, and The Muddlers Club), although delicious cuisine can be found across the region. In Derry, The Sooty Olive and Quaywest are both highlights, featuring meals made using locally sourced ingredients.

And, of course, you can't advocate cuisine in Northern Ireland without mentioning fish. St. George's Market in Belfast is the place to go for the freshest catch. However, shellfish and seafood may be found all along the coast.

5 - The villagers will treat you as if you were family.

The North of Ireland is noted for its céad mile fáilte, or "a hundred thousand welcomes." Northern Irish people are natural hosts; they are kind and friendly and always have a tale to tell. They have an uncanny capacity to make you feel at ease and at home. Family values and a feeling of community are at the heart of life in the North, and you'll remember this compassion and kindness long after you've returned home.

When you go to Northern Ireland with Trafalgar, you'll have plenty of opportunities to embrace the Giant Spirit of the region and meet some of the lovely people who live here. These are just a few of the locals that can't wait to meet you...

Map of Northern Ireland

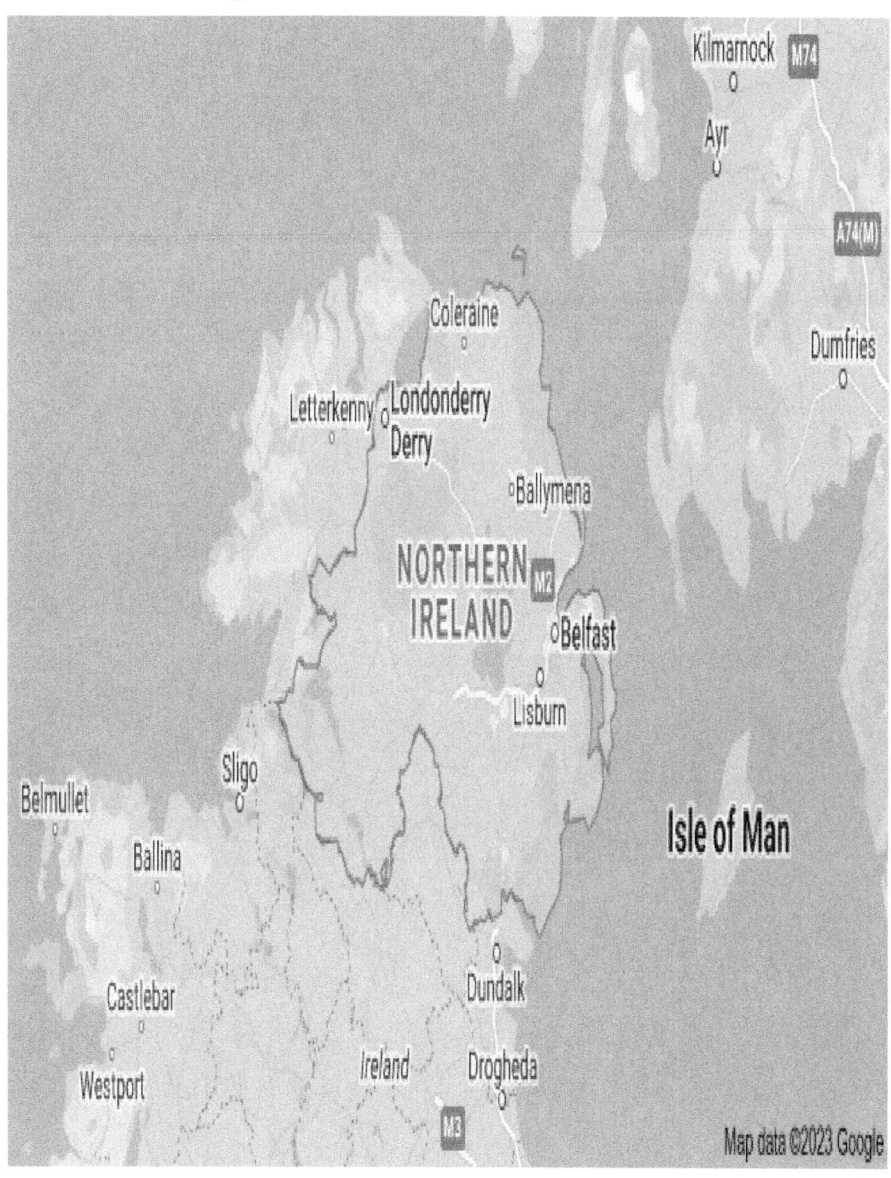

Chapter 2

The Best Time To Visit

We spend a lot of time in the relentless heat of sunny Thailand, so the four different seasons celebrated in Northern Ireland are something we greatly miss. Spring, summer, autumn, and winter are the four seasons.

While most people consider the summer months to be the greatest time to visit Northern Ireland, I believe that each season has its own set of perks and drawbacks.

While the summer months feature more daylight hours and nicer weather, they are also the busiest and draw the most tourists. The optimum time to visit Northern Ireland is determined by personal interests and the reasons for visiting Northern Ireland in the first place. Check out our road trip movie featuring Northern Ireland's finest for inspiration.

Northern Ireland in the Spring

After the gloomy weather of winter, the beginning of the tourism season in Northern Ireland is marked by the reopening of several tourist sites, including the different gardens and tours offered by the National Trust.

The leaves return to the trees in spring, flowers begin to blossom, the weather and gloomy sky improve, and it's just a lovely time to visit Northern Ireland.

Sheep in their infancy. The weather is still sporadic, but daylight hours are increasing, and the environment is improving as we approach summer. The woodland parks, which are normally damp, muddy, and neglected throughout the winter months, are also fantastic places to visit.

When does Spring arrive in Northern Ireland? Spring in Northern Ireland starts on March 1st, continues through April, and ends at the end of May. It is the time of year when animals and plants begin to awaken after a long winter.

Hillsborough Castle and Gardens, Mount Stewart, and Rowallane Gardens are the best tourist attractions in Northern Ireland in the spring.

Northern Ireland in the summer

Summer in Northern Ireland means t-shirt weather, and with the long summer vacations, people are out on the streets and in the pubs to soak up some rays while they can.

There will be activities practically every day around the nation, and with the bright weather and late daylight hours, it is the ideal time to go out and see the country.

However, the major beauty sites in Northern Ireland are busiest during the summer, so we normally avoid the Causeway Coast and other prominent tourist areas during this time owing to crowds and restricted parking.

The same can be said for nearby beaches like Crawfordsburn Country Park, which is popular with day-trippers who take the train down from Belfast.

But, at this time of year, there are innumerable quirky and outdoor experiences to be discovered in Northern Ireland's highlands and forest areas.

When does Summer arrive in Northern Ireland? Summer in Northern Ireland starts on June 1st, continues through July, and ends at the end of August.

Northern Ireland in Autumn

Autumn, or 'fall' for Americans, is a contrasting season since September is unquestionably one of the greatest months to visit Northern Ireland during the summer shoulder season. This is when the schools have returned, the crowds at big beauty areas have thinned, and the weather is still warm/mild enough to go exploring.

Outside of the main tourist months, accommodation in Northern Ireland is also less expensive and more plentiful. But then comes October, when the temperatures drop and the daylight hours become much shorter.

However, fall in Northern Ireland is a wonderful time to visit the parks and gardens as the leaves change color before Halloween.

> **When does Autumn arrive in Northern Ireland?** Autumn in Northern Ireland starts on September 1st, continues through October, and ends at the end of November. It is the time of year when plants and vegetation lose their leaves, and animals hibernate for the winter.

Northern Ireland in the winter

The holiday season begins in Northern Ireland not long after Halloween, with the traditional Christmas lights switching on and ornaments coming up around late to mid-November.

Then it's all smiles till the New Year, and there's the Belfast Christmas Market right in the heart of the city.

Otherwise, the weather is gloomy till spring, there are few bright hours, and I wouldn't advocate visiting Northern Ireland in winter. It also seldom snows (see video of Bangor below); however, snow may be seen on higher territory in the Mourne Mountains. Otherwise, interior amenities, such as Belfast's historic bars and pubs, make the city an attractive choice for a winter trip.

When does winter arrive in Northern Ireland? Winter in Northern Ireland starts on December 1st, continues through January, and ends at the end of February.

Travel Tips to Know Before Visiting

Northern Ireland is lush, attractive, and undiscovered. The following are genuine travel advice that will make exploring Northern Ireland a reality.

Money

Northern Ireland is a component of the United Kingdom, and its currency is the Pound Sterling, or £. (If you're going to the Republic of Ireland, you'll need Euros, €.) It's a good idea to visit your home bank several weeks before you go and order some Pounds Sterling to have on hand when you land.

If you don't have time, there are lots of businesses in the airport where you can exchange US dollars for British pounds—the fee is merely somewhat more than what your bank would charge you. Before traveling from Northern Ireland to England, convert your notes to Bank of England at any Bank of Ireland.

ATM's

There are ATM (cash) machines in cities and bigger towns where you may receive Pounds.

These are known as a "cashpoint," "cash machine," "hole in the wall," or "bankomat." (ATMs that are not run by banking institutions are referred to as "white-label" ATMs.) Cash machines may be found at banks, grocery shops, motels, and petrol stations.

They are also often seen at post offices in small towns. Before you go, notify your credit card or debit card issuers that you will be traveling to Northern Ireland. Remembering your PIN digits is also essential.

Cards de crédit

MasterCard and Visa credit cards are almost universally accepted. Prepaid cards, American Express cards, and traveler's checks are less frequent.

VAT Tax Credit

International visitors visiting the United Kingdom, including Northern Ireland, may refund VAT on any goods and services bought but not consumed in the United Kingdom.

It is now 20%. The VAT tax is included in the price of the item you buy. You are eligible for a VAT refund for the VAT you paid while traveling.

The majority of shops have a "tax-free shopping" sign in their window. When making a purchase, request a tax-free coupon. When you arrive at your departing airport, go to a VAT window (there are several) and present your coupons. Your coupons for a refund will be validated by a customs officer.

Electricity

Northern Ireland uses the same adaptor plugs as England—type G power sockets with three-pronged, rectangular pins.

Their voltage is double that of the United States. Simply buy an adaptor for your plug before you go.

They are cheap, compact, and simple to get online or in a variety of locations. If you forget, you can get one in Northern Ireland, but it's far simpler to obtain one ahead of time!

Chauffeured Transportation

Many individuals prefer to travel with a chauffeured driver. It is fairly priced, ideal for groups of many people traveling together, has space for your baggage, and allows you to relax and enjoy your holiday.

A local driver may also offer off-the-beaten-path options with you. Inquire with your Authentic Destination Expert about this possibility.

Northern Ireland Driving Yourself

All drivers must have their automobile rental insurance documentation and driver's license with them at all times.

Distances are indicated in miles and kilometers (km) on road signage in both English and Irish. Drive on the left side of the road. When approaching a roundabout, yield to traffic on the right.

(As in the United States, stop for emergency vehicles.) Passing must be done in the outside or right lane.

If you drive while wearing glasses or contacts, you must carry at least one set of backup corrective lenses with you.

Seatbelts are required to be worn at all times. Children under the age of 12 must be restrained in accordance with their age and stature.

Unless you have a hands-free device, do not use your mobile phone while driving. The legal BAC limit is 08%, and the consequences are severe if your BAC surpasses that figure.

Distances Traveled

Northern Ireland's speed limits are marked in mph and are the absolute maximum you should drive on any given route. To calculate your safe rate of speed, pay special attention to the weather and road conditions. In most urban locations, the speed restriction is up to 30 mph.

Outside of built-up regions, the speed limit is 60 mph. The speed limit on highways is 70 miles per hour. In congested locations, 20 mph is becoming the norm. Relax and enjoy the scenery. They are enthralling.

- **Dublin to Belfast**: 106 miles, 2 hours
- **Belfast to Derry**: 72 miles, 1.5 hours
- **Derry to Dublin**: 147 miles, 3.25 hours
- **Derry to the Giant's Causeway (Portrush):** 36 miles, 55 minutes
- **Giant's Causeway (Portrush) to Dublin**: 164 miles, 3 hours
- **Belfast to Galway**: 229 miles, 3.5 hours
- **Belfast to Enniskillen**: 82 miles, 1.5 hours

GPS

We highly advise using a GPS. When booking your vehicle rental, tell your Authentic Travel Expert that you want one. If you forget, you may acquire one at the rental agency counter at the airport. However, it is essential to prepare ahead of time.

Highway Signs

There are road signs in both English and Irish.

Marketplaces

Northern Ireland is a paradise for people who like shopping markets. St. George's Market in Belfast is an institution, one of the city's oldest marketplaces, featuring everything you can imagine under one roof. Organic vegetables, preserves, fresh baked foods, upcycled items, honey, crafts, textiles, jewelry, and pottery are available at Ards Artisans. It's located in Newtownards, around 11 miles from Belfast.

The Bangor Market in Bangor is one of Northern Ireland's major open-air marketplaces. The North Down Craft Collective, located just four miles from Belfast, features inspired crafts and delicacies with inexpensive handcrafted items.

Let the good times roll!

Todd's Leap Activity Centre in County Tyrone is suitable for people of all ages. It contains Granda Ben's Ethical Zoo Trail, where you may dig for fossils, visit the Dino park, or stroll through the forest for a zoo trip. Archery, a climbing wall, and a large swing are all available at Todd's Leap's Activity Centre.

High and extreme ziplines, paintballing, rope walks, clay pigeon shooting, and archery are all available. Skytrek by moonlight, River Adventure Packages, Nature Heritage Walks, and a Trakman Driving Range are all available at Colin Glen's Forest Flyover Zipline, which is just 6 miles from Belfast.

Consider the Crannagh Activity Centre on the north coast for watersports enthusiasts. Waterskiing, wakeboarding, stand-up paddleboarding, kayaking, and canoeing are among the activities available.

Far and Wild in Londonderry is the place to go for wild salmon kayaking, moonlight kayaking, and Giant's Causeway kayaking. To experience the tranquil heart of Fermanagh, hire a boat from Castle Archdale Boat Hire and explore the lakes.

Tipping

There was a time when no service workers in Europe expected or desired a gratuity.

And tipping someone who provided you with outstanding service and a nice chat is only basic politeness. Here is a rough guideline; however, as in the United States, go up or down based on the service you get.

- Waiters: 10% – 15%
- Hotel Porter: 1 Pound/bag
- Housekeeping: 1 Pound/day
- Concierge: 1 – 3 Pounds
- Taxi Driver: Please round up to the closest Pound.

Shop and Bank Hours

On Sundays, most large stores are open from 1 p.m. until 6 p.m. Most locations are open from 9 a.m. to 6 p.m.

Monday through Saturday. These hours may be lowered or expanded in small towns, depending on the owner's personal schedule.

Banks are typically open from 10:00 a.m. to 12:30 p.m. and 1:30 p.m. to 4:00 p.m., Monday through Friday. Post Office hours are 9 a.m. to 5:30 p.m., with certain offices closing for lunch.

Smoking, drugs, and alcohol

Smoking is prohibited in all public areas, including bars, restaurants, and shopping centers.

You may smoke outside where it is clearly marked as authorized. Possession of illicit substances is unlawful and may result in a jail term. The 08% legal limit for Blood Alcohol Content is carefully enforced.

Zone of time

In the summer, Northern Ireland observes Irish Standard Time (one hour ahead of Greenwich), and in the winter, Greenwich Mean Time.

Wireless Internet and Cell Phones

There are free hotspots accessible in major towns and cities. Your accommodations feature Wi-Fi, although connectivity is patchy in small towns, as it is elsewhere. Contact your mobile phone provider before you leave.

Most will charge you a nominal price, generally $10 per day, to make calls back to the United States and inside Northern Ireland on your mobile phone. This is quite useful!

Emergency Phone Number

Dial 112 for an emergency.

Health

Drugs and medications are sold in pharmacies, which are often known as "Chemists." On the street, look for a green cross on a white backdrop or a black wooden pole with a snake coiling around it. Most modest medical products are available at even the tiniest pharmacy store. If you need medical treatment, request that the hotel owner or concierge contact a General Practitioner on your behalf.

ID

At the airport automobile rental counter, you will need your US driver's license. If you want to drive into Northern Ireland, you will need your driver's license and/or passport.

How To Get To Northern Ireland

This guide will help you figure out how to travel from Dublin to Belfast, whether you're arriving from the UK mainland or flying in from another European nation.

How to Get to Northern Ireland By Air

Belfast International / Aldergrove and George Best/City Airport are our two airports. Despite the 'international,' the area receives few international flights.

Belfast International (previously known as Aldergrove) mostly serves Northern Irish tourists traveling to locations in the Mediterranean and Europe, as well as the UK mainland.

The majority of international tourists arrive at Dublin Airport or Shannon Airport in the Republic of Ireland or at an international airport in England, where visitors either drive up from the Republic or take a short domestic flight from England, landing at Belfast International or George Best/City Airport.

Domestic travelers going from other regions of the UK will find reasonably cheap flights to Belfast International or George Best/Belfast City Airport.

Belfast International Airport

- Address: Airport Road/A57, near Killealy, Antrim, BT29 4AB
- Phone: 028 9448 4848
- Website: www.belfastairport.com

Belfast International Airport (IATA: BFS, ICAO: EGAA) is approximately 21 kilometers / 13 miles from the city center. This may be a problem for Belfast City inhabitants, but it is not a problem for tourists heading up to the Causeway Coast to see attractions such as Giant's Causeway since it brings you that much closer.

In reality, given Northern Ireland's tiny area, the location of Belfast International Airport is unlikely to be a problem for anybody renting a vehicle and wants to go East, West, North, or

South. Furthermore, automobile rental rates are often lower when picked up at Belfast International.

How to get to and from Belfast International Airport: For people without a vehicle, there is a frequent express bus service that takes around 25 minutes to go into Belfast. Sit upstairs and take in the sights of our lush green landscape. There are bus services to Lisburn and Derry Londonderry as well. Check out Translink's website or the airport's 'to & from' page for further information.

George Best City Airport

- Location: Airport Road, Sydenham Bypass/A2, Belfast, BT3 9JH
- Tel: 02890 939093
- Web: www.belfastcityairport.com

George Best Airport (IATA: BHD, ICAO: EGAC) is mostly a local airport serving other cities in the United Kingdom, although there are also infrequent flights to/from Amsterdam and seasonal flights to overseas vacation spots. The airport is just 3 miles / 5 kilometers from Belfast's city center and stands near Belfast Lough.

Getting to and from George Best / City Airport: Public transportation is inadequate. There is a half-hour express bus service, although most people will use a cab or rent a vehicle. While Sydenham train station is touted as being a short distance' from the airport, you would need to drag your baggage for roughly 15-20 minutes down a walkway parallel to dual traffic before dragging them across a footbridge before arriving at the train station. Budget for a cab or rent a vehicle, in our opinion.

How to get to Northern Ireland from the Republic by Car, Bus, or Train

Driving

As previously said, many foreign visitors (and even residents) fly into Dublin Airport (which has, in our view, the greatest airport Twitter account) or Shannon Airport in the west and drive north. The border between the Republic of Ireland (ROI) and Northern Ireland (NI) is now open and is expected to remain so.

You can just drive over if you are authorized to do so. Check the details below to discover whether you need a visa to enter either ROI or NI.

The drive over the border is normally inconspicuous, but keep in mind that the conventional unit of measurement in the ROI is kilometers, whereas it is miles in Northern Ireland. Check your speed and keep in mind that depending on where you are, speed warnings will be in kilometers or miles!

If you are concerned about driving on the 'wrong' side of the road, keep in mind that the driver should always be in the center of the road. If the route is so narrow that this does not work, you have additional issues to deal with!

Vehicle Rental

We use Discovercars.com* for vehicle rental since it searches a wide variety of firms and returns cheap rates. It also has a high rating of 4.6 out of 5 on TrustPilot (with over 100,000 reviews). You may rent a vehicle in both the Republic and Northern Ireland and tour the whole island.

Make sure to notify the firm that you intend to travel borders so that you are properly insured. When you look for and choose a vehicle, an estimate of the extra cost appears under the 'Planning to travel to another country? Page.

By bus

There are frequent bus connections connecting Dublin Airport and the city center to Belfast and Derry Londonderry.

Translink, Northern Ireland's public transportation provider, provides bus service between Belfast/Derry Londonderry and Dublin/Dublin Airport for roughly £18 return if you book early to take advantage of a web saving rate.

There are pauses along the way, so the travel takes around 2 hours 15 minutes (Dublin Airport to Belfast) and a little less than four hours (Dublin to Derry Londonderry). If you have an early flight, there is a decreased service until the early hours of the morning.

Aircoach - In addition to serving several communities in the Republic, Aircoach also goes from Dublin city/airport to Belfast City (Glengall Street), Belfast International Airport, and Derry

Londonderry. A nonstop flight from Dublin Airport T1 and T2 to Belfast takes around 1 hour 50 minutes. Return tickets cost between £19 and £21, depending on the time of day. Tickets may be purchased online.

Taking the train

The train ride from Dublin Connolly to Belfast Lanyon Place takes little more than two hours. If your travel begins in the Republic, purchase tickets on the Irish Rail website; if it begins in Northern Ireland, book tickets on the Translink website.

You may also purchase tickets at the station, but buying online will save you the most money. Return ticket rates from Dublin may be as low as €28 (about) if you book early and get the saver seats, but otherwise, expect to spend approximately €30 or €32 for semi-flexible / flexible return tickets.

How to get to Northern Ireland by Sea

There are ferry services from Liverpool and Cairnryan in Scotland to Belfast, as well as an extra route from Cairnryan to Larne. There is a ferry service from the Isle of Man, so if you are going to the Isle of Man TT, why not come here after?

As with land and air travel, you may take a boat from the United Kingdom or Europe to the Republic of Ireland and then drive north from there.

Current ferry routes include:

- Cairnryan, Scotland - Larne, Northern Ireland (P&O Ferries)
- Cairnryan, Scotland - Belfast, Northern Ireland (Stena Line)
- Liverpool, England - Belfast, Northern Ireland (Stena Line)
- P&O Ferries, Liverpool, England - Dublin, Republic of Ireland
- Isle of Man Steam Packet Ferries from Douglas to Belfast
- Pembroke (Wales) - Rosslare (Ireland) (Irish Ferries)
- (Stena Line) Fishguard, Wales - Rosslare, Republic of Ireland
- Irish Ferries / Stena Line: Holyhead, Wales - Dublin, Republic of Ireland
- Irish Ferries connects Cherbourg, France, with Dublin, Republic of Ireland.
- Cherbourg (France) - Rosslare (Ireland) (Brittany Ferries / Stena Line)
- (Brittany Ferries) Roscoff, France - Cork, Republic of Ireland
- (Brittany Ferries) Roscoff, France - Rosslare, Republic of Ireland
- (Brittany Ferries) Bilbao, Spain - Rosslare, Republic of Ireland

Prices may be found at https://www.directferries.co.uk/.

Visa requirements and customs regulations

Before you embark on your exciting adventure, understanding visa requirements and customs regulations is crucial for a smooth and stress-free journey. This section will guide you through everything you need to know to enter and explore Northern Ireland with confidence.

Visa Requirements:

The Common Travel Area:

The good news for many travelers is that Northern Ireland, as part of the United Kingdom, operates within the Common Travel Area (CTA).

This means citizens of several countries, including most Commonwealth nations, EU and EFTA members, and Ireland, can visit, work, and study in Northern Ireland without a visa for up to 6 months. You simply need a valid passport. However, to ensure hassle-free entry, here are some key points to remember:

- **Passport Validity**: Your passport must be valid for the entire duration of your stay.
- **Proof of Funds**: Immigration officials may ask for evidence of sufficient funds to cover your intended stay.
- **Purpose of Visit:** Be prepared to explain the purpose of your visit, whether it's tourism, visiting family, or attending a conference.

- **Entry Refusal:** While unlikely, the right to enter the CTA lies with the border agent, and entry can be refused based on various factors.

Non-CTA Citizens

If you are not a citizen of a CTA country, you will likely need a visa to visit Northern Ireland. The type of visa required depends on your nationality, purpose of visit, and planned duration of stay. The UK Visas and Immigration (UKVI) website provides a handy visa checker tool to determine your specific visa requirements and guide you through the application process. Common visa types for Northern Ireland include:

- **Standard Visitor Visa**: For tourism, visiting family, and short-term business trips.
- **Transit Visa:** If you're just passing through Northern Ireland on your way to another country.
- **Work Visa**: If you plan to work in Northern Ireland.
- **Student Visa**: If you want to study in Northern Ireland.

Important Note: Visa requirements are subject to change, so always check the UKVI website for the latest information before your trip.

Customs Regulations:

After navigating the visa process, your next hurdle is customs. Knowing what you can and cannot bring into Northern Ireland will ensure a smooth passage through customs and avoid potential fines or confiscations. Here are some key points to remember:

Goods Allowed:

- Personal belongings: Clothes, toiletries, electronic devices for personal use, and reasonable amounts of medication are generally allowed duty-free.
- Food and drink: You can bring limited quantities of certain food and drink items for personal consumption, but restrictions apply to some animal products like meat and dairy. Check the latest guidance from the UK's Border Force website for specifics.
- Gifts: Gifts with a total value below £39 can be brought in duty-free.
- Tobacco and alcohol: Allowances are in place for tobacco and alcohol products. These vary depending on your age and whether you are arriving from within the EU or outside. Again, check the Border Force website for details.

Goods Prohibited:

- Illegal drugs and firearms: This one's a no-brainer but worth mentioning.

- Counterfeit goods: Don't try your luck with fake designer items or pirated items.

- Certain food items: Restrictions apply to some fresh fruits, vegetables, plants, and animal products due to biosecurity concerns.

- Endangered species and their products: Trade in such items is strictly prohibited.

Declarations:

- Goods exceeding allowances: If you are bringing in goods exceeding the allowed limits, you must declare them to customs and may be liable for duty.
- Cash: Carrying more than £10,000 in cash requires you to declare it at customs.

Online Pre-declaration:

To expedite your customs clearance, consider using the UK's Pre-Declaration Scheme for commercial goods. This allows you to submit your customs declaration online before arrival, potentially saving time at the border.

Important Resources:

- UK Visas and Immigration (UKVI): https://www.gov.uk/government/organisations/uk-visas-and-immigration
- UK Border Force: https://www.gov.uk/government/organisations/border-force
- Northern Ireland Tourist Board: https://discovernorthernireland.com/

Remember, a little preparation goes a long way! By understanding visa requirements and customs regulations before you travel, you can enter Northern Ireland with confidence and focus on creating lasting memories on your Irish adventure.

Chapter 3

Accommodation options in Northern Ireland

In our experience, short-stay accommodations are best booked via Booking.com* since breakfast is often included, payment is postponed until closer to your departure date, and cancellation policies are typically more flexible. Furthermore, when renting via the next best choice, AirBnB, you are often charged cleaning costs, which may be costly if you are just staying for a few days.

Estimated Fees for Accommodation

- Budget: Northern Ireland has various hostels with communal toilets ranging from 20 to 40 pounds per night, depending on where you travel.
- Mid-Range: Expect to spend between 80 and 120 pounds a night in a mid-range hotel. Northern Ireland boasts a wide range of bed and breakfast options.
- High-end B&Bs and hotels will cost between 150 and 200 pounds per night.

Accommodation in Belfast

Belfast's city center is tiny and centered around City Hall. In general, there are two clusters of hotels: one around Great Victoria Street Station, near the beautiful Opera House and iconic bars like The Crown Bar and Robinsons, and the other in and around the Cathedral Quarter, with its abundance of bars and restaurants.

There are also a few hotels with views of the Lagan. Because the city is tiny, it only takes 15-20 minutes to walk through the center, so no matter where you go, you will never be too far away from a restaurant, bar, or attraction.

Consider the lush alleys of Botanic & Queen's Quarters in and around Queen's University, the Botanic Gardens, and the Ulster Museum as you go out from the city center. The neighborhood is on the hop-on hop-off bus line, and a short walk/taxi ride into town.

Accommodation Recommendation. >>

The city center

- **The Europa,** sometimes known as 'the world's most bombed hotel,' is a landmark in Belfast. Despite its past, it has recently been rebuilt and deserves to be regarded as one of Belfast's greatest hotels.
- **The Merchant Hotel -** anticipates opulence and history, as well as proximity to the Cathedral Quarter's bars and restaurants.
- **The Bullitt Hotel** - The Bullitt Hotel is a sibling hotel of the Merchant and is likewise situated in the Cathedral Quarter. The hotel is named after Steve McQueen's 1968 film Bullitt, and the mood is appropriately McQueen cool.
- **Titanic Quarter** - next to Titanic Belfast and occupies the former Harland & Wolff Offices of the old shipyard where Titanic was constructed. Remember that it is situated across the river from the city center, although it is only a

short walk or taxi ride away. Excellent news for George Best Airport. Find out more >>

Botanic Gardens / Queen's Quarter

- **Gregory by the Warren Collection** is a reasonably priced hotel with a garden in Queen's Quarter's lush streets. While there are no breakfast or eating facilities, there are several cafés and restaurants nearby.
- • **The 1852 Hotel** - A self-check-in hotel with spacious rooms and comfortable mattresses, as well as an excellent restaurant/café below. A unique greeting with a complimentary drink! Find out more >>

Accommodation on the Causeway Coast and Glens

Most sites are a short day-trip away from any spot along the Causeway Coast, so you can select a place to stay that matches your requirements without being concerned about being in the 'wrong' place.

Ballycastle (for Rathlin Island, traditional pubs, the Dark Hedges, and the Glens), Bushmills (for the distillery and the Giant's Causeway), and Portrush and Portstewart (for beaches, restaurants, and other attractions) are the primary places to stay in. Cushenden and Cushendall in the Glens, as well as Ballintoy, Dunseverick, Portballintrae, and Castlerock, are all worth a visit.

There are many beautiful locations to stay in rural settings around the coast, the Glens, and the region near Benevenegh and Limavady, as well as farther inland along the Bann River.

Last but not least, we must recommend the Causeway Hotel, which is just next to the Giant's Causeway and offers fantastic views of the coast as well as free entrance to the Giant's Causeway center (the Causeway itself is always free).

Accommodation in Derry Londonderry

DerryLondonderry is famed for its walls, and there are many hotels and B&Bs inside the city walls if you want to be right in the middle of all the history. Parking may be an issue, but since the city is so small, you may simply park outside the city limits and stroll. Municipal carparks are the most cost-effective alternative, and they are the easiest to use using the Just Park app, which enables you to fill them out remotely.

Outside the city walls, towards the university, there are a number of hotels and B&Bs.

Accommodation Recommendation

Within the city limits

- **Number eight ££The Townhouse,** A Victorian-inspired bed & breakfast. (Rating 9.0 on Booking.com)
- **££ Shipquay Boutique Hotel is a** magnificent and cozy boutique hotel housed in a historic structure. (Rating 9.0 on Booking.com)
- **Hotel Maldron City ££** A contemporary 4-star hotel located inside the city walls. Some rooms feature views of the River Foyle and the surrounding walls. (Rating 8.2 on Booking.com)
- **££££ Bishop's Gate Hotel** is another ancient luxury boutique hotel inside the city walls, this time housed in a beautiful listed structure from the 1800s. (Rating 9.2 on Booking.com)

Near the city walls

- **The Jazz House £ and The Art House $** Both owned by the same firm, these townhouse hotels are lavishly designed in an Edwardian / Roaring Twenties style. A quiet residential street near the university is just outside

the city walls. Breakfast is not included. (Booking.com rating 9.3 / 9.5)
- **Holiday Inn Express ££** This well-known hotel chain offers few surprises. Just beyond the city gates, it is a decent 3-star contemporary hotel. Breakfast is served as a buffet. (Rating 8.4 on Booking.com)

City outskirts (easy parking)

- **Arkle home** is a charming rural home with grounds, parking, and a delicious breakfast. (Booking.com rating 9.1) Everglades Hotel £ A contemporary 4-star hotel over the River Foyle with views of Donegal's hills. (Rating 8.7 on Booking.com) Larchmont House B&B £££ A friendly Grade II-listed Georgian home located on lovely grounds, with a delicious breakfast included. (Booking.com rating 9.8)

Accommodation in Fermanagh Lakelands

Fermanagh has several great locations to stay, and where you stay will be determined by how you choose to spend your time - Enniskillen is the major town with restaurants and taverns, although you may opt to stay lakeside or in the country to enjoy the landscape and tranquillity.

Accommodation Recommendation

- **Belmore Court ££** A functional new hotel only 10 minutes' walk from Enniskillen's town center, with delicious breakfasts. (Booking.com rating 8.8) Dromard House £ A friendly B&B in a peaceful rural location two miles from Enniskillen. The accommodation is in an annex with a guest kitchen, and breakfast is provided in the main house. A stroll through the woods leads to the lough's coast. (Booking.com rating 9.4)

- **Ashwoods House** £ A rural location on the route to Cuilcagh, Marble Arch Caves, and Florence Court, just outside Enniskillen. Each room has a kitchenette and a terrace with garden views. Breakfast is highly regarded. (Rating 9.8 on Booking.com)
- **Lakeside Hotel & Lodges Killyhevlin £££** A contemporary resort hotel on the lough coast just outside of Enniskillen featuring a spa, gym, indoor pool, two restaurants, and a bar. (8.5 out of 10 on Booking.com)
- **£££ Lough Erne Resort** The 2013 G8 summit was held at this 5-star luxury hotel, which has two championship golf courses, a Thai spa, an infinity pool, extensive grounds, and all suites with lake views. A short distance from Enniskillen. (Rating 8.7 on Booking.com)

South Down Accommodation - St. Patrick's Country and the Mournes

You should look for accommodation in or around Newcastle or Downpatrick since the attractions highlighted in our guide to the region are all nearby. The Slieve Donard Hotel and Spa in Newcastle offers a wide choice of accommodations, from glamping pods with stunning views to 4-star grandeur.

Accommodation Recommendation

- **Conlin House is located in Newcastle. ££:** A Newcastle seaside Bed and breakfast with sea views and easy access to the town's cafes and restaurants. Complete Irish breakfast!
- **Newcastle's Slieve Donard Hotel & Spa ££££:** A landmark four-star Victorian hotel nestled on six acres of pristine private gardens by the sea with views of the Mournes.
- **The Dundrum Inn is located in Dundrum. ££:** An 18th-century inn with a garden, café, and bar, so you won't have to go far to have your first Guinness.
- **Denvir's Coaching Inn, Downpatrick ££:** Denvir's is Ireland's oldest surviving Coaching Inn and is now a grade 'A' listed property. It is within walking distance of St. Patrick's Centre, graveyard, and other attractions.

Northern Ireland has 10 beautiful places to stay.

When it comes to selecting the ideal staycation, you might be excused for being dissatisfied with hotels and basic self-catering accommodations.

Many individuals in Northern Ireland who are vacationing at home are increasingly seeking somewhere to stay with a distinctive twist.

From refurbished cathedrals and glamping pods to bubbles and castles, the nation is full of strange and beautiful locations to spend the night.

Here are some suggestions for unusual and intriguing locations to visit this year:

1. Castlerock's Burrenmore Nest

Burrenmore Nest's lodges each include a king-size bed, a private hot tub, and a campfire. With an in-room projector, you can even organize your own movie night.

Alternatively, grab yourself a drink and relax in the surrounding woodland. Each tree-top cabin comes with a reclaimed wood coffee table, a kitchenette, an ensuite bathroom, and thermostat heating. This site is solely for adults and features two pet-friendly lodges.

- https://www.burrenmore-nest.com/
- **Address**: 5 Burrenmore Rd, Castlerock, Coleraine BT51 4SA, United Kingdom

2. Coleraine's The Oat Box

Using reused materials and the original mahogany floor, this converted 1968 TK horse truck has been transformed into a magnificent and serene sanctuary nestled on private farmland. The cottage can accommodate two individuals and is an ideal base for exploring the north shore.

Enjoy the designated outdoor area and take a climb to the top of the hill on-site for some stunning views over Mussenden and Inishowen. To help you feel at home, there is a full-size shower, a two-ring electric stove, and a small oven.

- **Address**: 30 A, 30 Rectory Rd, Coleraine BT52 2LS, United Kingdom

3. Strangford's Quarry Hill Church

This venue will undoubtedly give a once-in-a-lifetime experience. The church has been lovingly repaired and transformed into lovely self-catering lodging. With a traditional blue façade and a stone floor dating back to 1846, this airy and attractive place with an open-plan communal area is sure to wow.

The structure features five bedrooms, four of which have ensuite bathrooms, as well as a family bathroom. Despite its antiquity, this property has contemporary heating and hot water systems, as well as a laundry room.

The garden has a grilling area as well as a sitting where you can listen to the cries of curlews and oyster catchers in the harbor. Individual consideration may be given to pets.

- quarryhillchurch.com
- **Address**: 56 Downpatrick Rd, Strangford, Downpatrick BT30 7LZ, United Kingdom

4. Cookstown's Sperrinview Glamping

Sperrin View Glamping is nestled in the foothills of the Sperrin Mountains. This astronomer's paradise is located in one of Northern Ireland's most gorgeous areas and is a Dark Sky location. It is an ideal location for outdoor activities due to its closeness to Davagh Forest, which has bike and walking routes.

There are two double beds and a couch bed in each pod/cabin. Guests get full access to the community center, which contains a fully equipped kitchen, a reading nook, and a veranda with an open fire from which to view the stars.

- sperrinviewglamping.com
- **Address**: 71 Blackrock Rd, Cookstown BT80 9PA, United Kingdom

5. Bangor's Helen's Tower

If you want to get away from it all for a while, here is the spot for you. Helen's Tower has panoramic views of the Scottish coast, the Isle of Man, and the Welsh highlands. This site has one double bedroom available for adults alone.

Visitors may take advantage of nearby walking trails or just unwind in their individual towers, perhaps with a book in the reading area or beside the open fire. This home has no WiFi, so prepare for a social media detox in this remote yet serene setting.

- irishlandmark.com/property/helens-tower
- **Address**: Clandeboye Rd, Bangor BT23 4RX, United Kingdom

6. Killough, JP Ketch

This distant and picturesque location will allow you to experience the life of a lightkeeper in a unique self-catering accommodation. Irish Lights repaired the lightkeepers' cottages, which are currently cared for by the Irish Landmark Trust.

Another Wifi-free area, this location is an excellent starting point for exploring the neighboring Strangford Lough and trekking.

There is one double bedroom, one twin bedroom, one bathroom, and a separate WC in this house. On the terrace outdoors, you may enjoy views of the sea.

- irishlandmark.com/property/jp-ketch
- **Address:** 1 and 3 The Lighthouse, Point Road, Saint John's Point, Killough, Downpatrick, Co Down,

7. Ballycastle Pod by the Pond / Bushmills

This pod is situated between the Northcoast villages of Bushmills and Ballycastle, only a short drive from Whitepark Bay. It offers a terrace and a garden area with a BBQ overlooking a pond.

An outhouse has a shower and toilet with hot water, as well as a double bed and a communal space in the main pod. Every visitor receives a free 20% discount coupon for Bothy Coffee, which is around two miles away from the pod.

- airbnb.co.uk
- **Address**: 57 Priestland Rd, Bushmills BT57 8UR, United Kingdom

8. Portglenone's Foxborough Bubble Den

This bubble den will provide every visitor with an amazing experience. The main area, a pressurized tent with a bedroom and toilet, offers views of the landscape and sky.

A complementary breakfast tray will provide you with a pleasant and rewarding start to the day after a night under the stars. Wifi is available.

- airbnb.co.uk
- **Address**: 170 Gortgole Rd, Ballymena BT44 8AS, United Kingdom

9. Markethill, Teepee Valley

Teepee Valley is a luxurious, family-friendly glamping camp. The majority of their rooms include fire pits. The Large Yurt is one of their accommodations, a cozy and roomy area perfect for larger families and parties.

A private stone shower room is located next door. The room has a double bed, a single-day bed, and two rollout mattress beds that may accommodate up to five people.

- tepeevalleycampsite.co.uk
- **Address**: 20 Shanecrackan Road, Markethill BT60 1TS, United Kingdom

10. Lisbellaw's Belle Isle

In this opulent 17th-century castle on a private Fermanagh isle, you may live out your own fairy tale. The Abercorn Wing and the Hamilton Wing are two of the castle's lodging choices for visitors. The castle can accommodate up to 26 guests.

The structure has a double-vaulted entry hall and a warm drawing room with floor-to-ceiling windows and a beautiful fireplace. Guests may explore the surrounding gardens and have access to boats that can be rented.

- belle-isle.com
- **Address**: Belle Isle Estate, Lisbellaw, Enniskillen BT94 5HG, United Kingdom

Getting Around Northern Ireland

Northern Ireland is easy to navigate, and since it is so tiny, it is also stress-free. We try our best to assist you in traveling to as many of our most popular sites and stunning landscapes as possible with decent roads, fantastic public transportation, and a variety of cheap passes.

Vehicle rental

It couldn't be simpler to get through Northern Ireland by car. You may bring your own automobile on the boats or rent one at the port of entry. Find the best automobile rental service here.

Just make sure you remember which side of the road you're on before you go. Here's a pro tip that applies everywhere. The line is always on the driver's side (as long as you're in the appropriate vehicle, of course), and for the first few hours, halt and ponder before making that turn at a junction.

Itineraries and tours

Taking a tour is a terrific way to go about without having to worry about anything, and Northern Ireland provides a wide choice of guided excursions to suit all interests. There is a trip for everyone, whether you want a literary, political, or pub tour, whether you want to go about by bus, taxi, boat, or foot. There are self-guided tours and itineraries available. View them all here.

Using a Taxi

Taxis are often the initial point of contact for guests, and they play an important role in greeting them and imparting their local knowledge of the region.

They might be a cost-effective solution for short trips. All licensed taxis in Northern Ireland must show taxi license plates.

Taxis and their services often give meter-reading prices; if a taxi does not have a meter, inquire about the fee to your location before departing.

Taxi ranks are also accessible in Belfast, usually in the city center or at ports of entrance. Visitors traveling with Guide Dogs may find further information.

Tours by Taxi

In fact, taxi services are so outstanding in this city that taking a cab tour has become almost mandatory. Our taxi drivers are never short of banter, and these trips provide a closer look at the region's recent history and politics.

They are offered by a variety of businesses in both Belfast and Derry-Londonderry and often include London-style black taxis - discover a taxi tour here.

Electric Bikes (electrically assisted pedal bikes) are being used in Northern Ireland.

To use an EAPC on public roads in Northern Ireland, an EAPC user must be at least 14 years old. Owners/riders should think about getting insurance to cover things like damage, theft, personal injury, and liability.

Owners of EAPCs in Northern Ireland are no longer needed to: • register, license, and insure EAPCs before using them on public highways, cycle paths, or anyplace else pedal cycles are permitted; or • wear a motorcycle helmet or carry a valid or full driving license.

Electric Vehicles (ecars) in Northern Ireland

Electric vehicles are seen as a step toward a more sustainable future, and the move may grow more enticing in the coming years. ecarNI has established a significant electric vehicle charging infrastructure in Northern Ireland, with over 300 charging outlets spread throughout several towns and cities.

Public transportation

Translink is Northern Ireland's primary public transportation company. Translink provides a variety of low-cost tickets, Smartcards, and mobile tickets to assist you in going throughout Northern Ireland by bus and train. To purchase mobile tickets, download the free mLink App from Google Play or the App Store.

Translink provides a variety of discounted and Senior Citizen passes for travel around Northern Ireland. Furthermore, with a valid 60+, Senior SmartPass, or RoI Senior SmartPass, all senior persons living in Northern Ireland and the Republic of Ireland may now enjoy free internal transit within both jurisdictions.

There are additional services that are very appealing to guests. The Rambler Bus Services are intended to increase the accessibility of our picturesque rural regions to visitors, walkers, and bikers. Call the Translink Contact Centre at (028) 90 66 66 30 for schedule information.

Ulsterbus Day excursions depart daily from the Europa Buscentre during the summer months (with limited programming at other times of the year) for a variety of guided excursions around Northern Ireland and beyond the border.

National Trust estates, beach resorts, retail locations, athletic and entertainment events, and unique seasonal journeys are among the destinations. Prices begin at £22.50.

Translink schedules and tariffs may be found at www.translink.co.uk or by calling the Contact Centre at (028) 90 66 66 30.

With a Metro dayLink card, you can explore Belfast at your leisure, with unlimited travel on the Metro network starting at £3.50 (fares subject to change).

You may fill your dayLink card with 1, 5, or 10 days of travel and use it anytime you wish.

The Belfast Visitor Pass is an integrated Translink smartcard that provides unrestricted bus and train travel inside the Belfast Visitor Pass Zone for 1, 2, or 3 consecutive days. It also offers a variety of appealing discounts at city attractions, excursions, leisure and retail stores, coffee shops, and restaurants.

It is suitable for both adults and children and is great for those who like to travel by bus and train and take advantage of the city's many offerings.

Northern Ireland Packing Essentials

Over multiple journeys, I spent nearly a month traveling around Ireland and Northern Ireland, seeing practically every county.

I've spent over twenty days on cross-country road trips, so I know what it's like to prepare for a variety of activities while living out of a bag.

I've also gone on luxury excursions to Dublin, staying in excellent hotels and being based in the city, so I've included recommendations for what to dress in Ireland that are appropriate for both the Wild Atlantic Way and fitting in while in Dublin and Belfast.

Here's my packing list for Ireland and Northern Ireland, which includes what to take for ladies and men in all seasons.

What Should I Bring in My Suitcase?

Planning your first vacation to Ireland and wondering what you definitely must pack? A vacation here might include a wide range of activities, so having a rough concept of your basic plan before you come can help you pack appropriately.

However, I've had extended car trips across the nation with drastically varied activities scheduled from day to day, so this packing list should be appropriate for whatever kind of vacation you'll be doing here. The first thing you must select is what kind of suitcase to bring.

Because I am secure in my packing judgments, the longer I travel, the smaller my luggage gets. I checked a large amount of luggage on my initial visits to Ireland. These days, I can comfortably live in my 48L backpack for a month (assuming I wash laundry in the sink or have access to laundry facilities).

You'll need to select whether to carry a roller suitcase or a backpack as your primary luggage. This is determined by a variety of things. If you want to be predominantly located in one location for an extended length of time, this option is less important. However, for someone who will be traveling from place to place on a regular basis, I prefer a backpack over a roller suitcase.

You must also determine if you will travel carry-on alone or with luggage. Both types of baggage are available in carry-on sizes. However, I know hikers whose bags are huge enough that they must be checked. Keep in mind that not all backpacks are carry-on-sized.

My personal choice is to use a carry-on-sized backpack since I often go to Ireland for extended periods of time (over two weeks) and like the flexibility that comes with not having too many things with me. While traveling between cities every few days, it's wonderful not to have too much to think about while visiting many places in succession.

On my most recent journey, I flew into Belfast and out of Dublin, stopping at Antrim, New Grange, Dingle, and Kerry along the way. This is a lot of hotel changes, even spaced out across two and a half weeks!

Questions to Consider When Choosing a Suitcase

- Do you have private or shared lodging?
- Do you intend to stay at a hostel where your bag must fit into a tiny locker?
- Which floor will you be staying on? Is an elevator available? Are you certain?
- How many hotel stays and transit days will be included in this trip?
- Do you tend to overpack and not utilize all of your belongings when you travel?

Once you've arrived in Ireland, you'll need a dependable and secure day bag to transport items such as your camera and wallet. This backpack is particularly useful for transportation days since it stores items that you need to access while on the go.

What to Look for in a Travel Day Bag

- The bag is fashionable enough that it does not scream "tourist."
- Safety elements that protect you from low-level crime aimed at tourists
- There should be enough space for the technology you're carrying, such as a laptop, tablet, camera, and so on.
- Wearable on lengthy days of sightseeing

- If your primary luggage is a carry-on, it will fit beneath an aircraft seat.
- Suitable for the kind of travel you're taking

How to Organize Your Bags

When traveling in Ireland and Northern Ireland, it is important to keep your belongings organized. When you need to open your luggage in public, everything has to be in its proper location so you can get in and out fast.

In cities, keeping your luggage open increases the danger of theft or accidentally losing anything. Both events occurred to me while traveling while I was not keeping my belongings properly arranged. It stinks, believe me!

Whatever luggage and day bag you choose, you'll need smaller organizing bags to keep everything in order. Here's what I bring with me on my trips:

- **Packing Cubes**: For clothing, I bring 1-2 big packing cubes and 1 smaller packing cube for underwear, bras, swimwear, and pajamas.
- **Little Cosmetic Bags**: I have five little cosmetic bags that I use to store various products. My make-up and jewelry, wet and dry toiletries, medical bag, and electronics bits and ends are all organized.
- I use the laundry bag that comes with my packing cubes.
- **Coin Purse**: Coins accumulate quickly, particularly in Ireland and Northern Ireland, where the money is more valuable than in the United States! Nothing is worse than discovering the equivalent of $10 USD in pennies as you

pack your belongings to depart, knowing that you're essentially throwing money away.
- **Canvas Tote Bag**: Ideal for grocery shopping, doing errands, or relaxing on lazy days.
- **Ziplock Bags:** These are fantastic! For odd organizing crises, I bring 1-2 empty gallon ziplock bags and 3-5 empty tiny ziplock bags. These tend to occur on every trip, and I'm always delighted to have them.

What Women Should Pack

What should women bring to Northern Ireland and Ireland? Consider what activities you'll be undertaking while choosing your outfit. Are you planning to see a play in Dublin? Are you going to hike the Ring of Kerry or stay in a rural house on the Antrim Coast? Are you going for a stroll along the Antrim Coast or a tea at a posh hotel?

Women in Dublin dress stylishly and casually. Wear what makes you feel good with breezy materials that dry quickly. This list implies you'll be on the road for more than a week and will hand-wash and hang-dry your items when you run out. If you're just going for a few days, carry less clothing.

Summer, Spring, and Autumn Clothes in Ireland

- Three to four shirts or blouses
- , one tank top
- 1 t-shirt
- 2-3 dresses (If you don't wear dresses or skirts, bring extra shirts and pants to substitute).

- Several pairs of leggings (optional). I like wearing leggings when traveling because they allow me to wear a gorgeous outfit while being quite comfortable, and they're wonderful for layering since Ireland can be cold in the early spring and late fall. The weather was pleasant in late September, but by the middle of October, it had become cold.
- a single pair of jeans
- 1 (optional) skirt
- 1 sweater, cardigan, or kimono for light layering (I discovered that even in May, I needed layers).
- 1 jacket (I packed my jean jacket, but anything that can withstand mild rain would also be a good idea given how often it rained throughout our two weeks).
- 1 pyjama set
- 1 pair of pajama bottoms (or one of the leggings)
- 1 swimsuit (depending on the weather and plans).

Sandals and Shoes

I bring three pairs of shoes with me when I travel. Two pairs of strong shoes for seeing the cities on long days and one pair of comfy slip-on jellies or sandals for when I return to my hotel or apartment.

- Comfortable Closed-Toed Walking Shoes (If hiking, I recommend Pack hiking shoes; otherwise, any closed-toed shoe will do). Long days walking on pavement or cobblestones are to be expected. My feet were utterly battered up by the conclusion of the day's touring.

- For cold weather months, I opt for the second pair of boots. Both the sandals and the boots are perfect for travel because the rubber souls make them extra durable and comfortable at the same time.
- Extra-easy slip-on sandals or flip-flops (I like Croc Jellies since they're great for hostel showers but also worn outdoors; I'm presently on pairs #2 and 3, and I have them in blue and pink).

Socks and underwear

- 7-8 pairs of underwear: I prefer to carry enough for a week's worth of washing, but you may bring more or less depending on your requirements.
- 1-2 bras: If you plan on doing a lot of hiking, one of them should be a sports bra.
- 1-2 bralettes: I started wearing them this year, and I'm enamored with them. They're practically as comfy as a light sports bra. Add a pair of bralettes to your baggage if you have bigger breasts and want to be able to relax at your hotel or hostel without feeling like you're dressed improperly.
- 7-8 pairs of socks: Even in the summer, when I'd like to wear sandals, I find myself requiring socks and boots in cities. Combining walking tours, lengthy days of travel, and public transit, I find that I need more support and, hence, extra socks.

Accessories and Jewelry

- 1-2 pieces of each kind of jewelry you like. That's a couple of sets of earrings, one bracelet, two rings, and a necklace for me.
- Sunglasses (normal or prescription if necessary). You'll be spending more time outdoors than you think in Ireland.
- Hairpins, Bobby Pins, or Barretts (1-3 styles per hair type)
- Headbands or hair wraps (1-4, depending on your requirements)
- (Optional) Watch

What Women Should Wear in Ireland in the Winter

Ireland is well-known for its warm winters, with temperatures averaging in the mid-forties. However, I notice that when I travel, I am always cooler than when I am at home at the same temperature. This is because I am outside for considerably longer amounts of time when I travel than I am during a typical day. So much of travel is appreciating and seeing natural wonders.

For example, last year, I spent four days in Dublin on a city break. Even though it was just mid-October, I found myself chilly while going about. So these suggestions are for someone who knows they'll be spending a lot of time outdoors on their vacation. If you're only visiting Dublin or Belfast for a brief city vacation and won't be spending much time outdoors, feel free to disregard any of these suggestions.

- **A Winter Coat:** You'll need one that can withstand the cold. It's a bit of an outlay, but you'll be glad you did.
- **Thermal Layers:** This will be on my packing list for any cold-weather travel. It's fantastic since you can wear it on its own for a fast layer of warmth or beneath your coat when it's extremely chilly outdoors.
- **Shoes**: Replace your ordinary city boots with waterproof ones.
- **Socks**: Replace your old socks with thick, toasty wool socks.
- **Gloves**: You'll be doing a lot of navigation on your smartphone in Dublin and Belfast, particularly while using public transportation. I found it really inconvenient to have to remove my gloves every few minutes, so I switched to tech-friendly gloves. They're also useful for taking images with your phone.
- **Winter Scarf:** You'll want a thick knit scarf that you can draw up and use to protect your face as needed.
- **Leggings**: When you're outdoors, you'll want to be covered from head to toe. Regular leggings are perfect for late fall, but for winter, change them out for fleece-lined leggings. You may wear them under dresses or even beneath jeans.
- **Hat**: A fleece-lined knit hat will keep you warm while also making you look like a local.

What Men Should Wear in Ireland

Men, like women, will want to dress in simple, elegant attire to blend in.

Summer, Spring, and Autumn Clothes in Ireland

The clothing you pack will be determined by the activities you want to participate in. A simple list will contain the following:

- 4-5 day-to-day tees
- 1 cuffed shirt
- three undershirts
- 1-2 pairs of shorts (summer only; avoid khaki or cargo shorts that seem excessively touristic).
- two pairs of jeans
- 1 pair of wrinkle-free dress pants (for doing anything good in the city)
- 1 rain-resistant light jacket
- 1 sleeping tee shirt and shorts
- 1 pair of swim trunks (optional, depending on the weather and your intentions)

Sandals and Shoes

- Closed-toed walking shoes that are comfortable (sneakers, hiking shoes, or boots, depending on your desire).
- Day sandals that are both comfortable and stylish. Bring a second pair of walking shoes if you are the kind of man who does not wear sandals.

- Extra-easy slip-on sandals or flip-flops (particularly vital for hostel guests).

Socks & Undies

- Approximately 7-8 pairs of undergarments
- Approximately 7-8 pairs of socks

Accessories and Jewelry

- Sunglasses (normal or prescription if necessary)
- (Optional) Watch
- Any kind of personal jewelry

What Men Should Wear in Winter

As I said in the part on what ladies should wear in Northern Ireland in winter, you should dress expecting it to feel colder than the weather forecast. Even while Ireland offers warm winters in the mid-forties, most tourist spots will seem considerably colder after spending hours outdoors touring. When you combine it with strong coastal gusts, it's a formula for being chilled to the bone.

- **A Winter Coat:** You'll need one that can withstand the elements. Because of the requirement of taking public transit in cities and seeing Ireland's natural beauty in the countryside, expect to spend a lot of time outside, even in winter.
- **Wool Baselayer:** A wool baselayer will provide additional warmth beneath your shirt.
- **Shoes:** Replace your ordinary city boots with waterproof ones.

- **Socks**: Replace your old socks with thick, toasty wool socks.
- **Gloves**: You'll be doing a lot of navigation on your smartphone in Ireland, particularly while using public transportation. I found it really inconvenient to have to remove my gloves every few minutes, so I switched to tech-friendly gloves. They're also useful for taking images with your phone.
- **Winter Scarf:** You'll want a thick knit scarf that you can draw up and use to protect your face as needed.
- **Hat**: A fleece-lined knit hat will keep you warm while also making you look like a local.

Skincare and toiletries

Not all of these apply to everyone, but here's a broad list of items I usually bring with me. Remember that if you're traveling carry-on only, all liquids must be in travel-sized bottles that fit into a transparent ziplock bag. The carry-on liquids allowance is 3.4oz (100ml).
- Bathing and hair care
- Shampoo and conditioner in travel size. Although some people swear by solid shampoo, I just refill the same travel-size bottles.
- Dry shampoo is great for days when you don't want to shower.
- Hairbrush for little hair
- If you're taking a hair dryer from North America, bring a voltage converter or a travel-sized hair dryer with an Ireland and Northern Ireland plug.
- Hair care products tailored to your hair type

- Soap
- Razor
- Optional Shaving Cream

Skincare

- Sunscreen
- Moisturizer (travel is harsh on the skin). Because you'll be spending so much time outdoors, an SPF moisturizer is ideal, but it's not a replacement for sunscreen.
- Night Cream to aid in skin recovery.
- Lotion for the body
- Deodorant
- Vaseline.
- Makeup
- Towelettes for removing makeup
- Dental Treatment
- Toothbrush
- Toothpaste
- Floss
- Eyecare
- Contacts, contact case, and solution (if applicable)
- Prescription glasses and sunglasses (if necessary)

Miscellaneous

- Travel Towel in Full Size. Most people I know despise their microfiber travel towels, but I chose a large, lovely microfiber towel that's ideal for the beach or a hostel. Nobody likes their travel towel as much as I do.
- Kleenex, Tissues, or Toilet Paper

- Hand Sanitizer in Travel Size for all those days spent on public transportation.
- File for Nails
- Clippers for Nails
- Tweezers (one pair for my beauty bag and one pair for my toiletry kit).
- Washing detergent powder (enough for 3-4 loads of washing; if I'm traveling for a longer period of time, I can always acquire more on the road).
- Something to help you get through that special time of the month. If you have to spend time on the road, pack anything you need based on your preferences.

Accessories and Technology

Here's the technology that I use when traveling.

- I use a MacBook Air as my laptop.
- Charger for a laptop
- Laptop Case
- Smart Phone (I have a Samsung8, which I adore; if you wish to pick up a sim card while in Ireland, make sure you have an unlocked phone; if it isn't already, your cell carrier can unlock it ahead of time).
- Phone Case (Using an OtterBox is like carrying your phone around in a pillow).
- Headphones. This is particularly crucial since you will be using a lot of public transportation.
- Cell Phone Charger
- Backup Power Bank
- DSLR or digital camera (I use a Nikon D810)

- Spare Camera Battery (I use the Nikon battery that comes with my camera).
- Charger for Camera Batteries
- SD Cards (I suggest at least one main and one backup).
- Dropbox Account for Photo Backup
- Two USB-enabled universal outlet adapters. Ireland and Northern Ireland utilize different plugs than continental Europe or North America. Remember that unless your North American appliances can withstand 220V, they will fry. Before using, double-check each one! So many hair dryers have burned out (including one in Galway)!
- Kindle Paperwhite for reading without carrying books around
- Kindle Case
- DJI Osmo Cell Phone Gimbal for videography. (Obviously, not for everyone, but if you want to shoot movies on your vacation, this gimbal will transform your life).

Documentation of Importance

- Are you thinking about renting a vehicle in Ireland? You'll need your driver's license as well as your passport!
- Your passport and either a soft copy or a handful of physical copies. Take it with you when you go to get a SIM card.
- Holder of a passport
- If you want to hire a vehicle in Ireland, bring your driver's license as a backup form of identification.
- Your Travel Insurance Policy: I never leave the house without travel insurance. You never know what type of

difficulty you'll encounter when driving. I've had multiple shattered phones, an almost stolen wallet, vehicle rental mishaps, and other mishaps. I pay for World Nomads and enthusiastically suggest them. I always acquire a higher level so that I can protect more of my electronics in the event that it is lost or stolen. It is particularly vital to have travel insurance if you want to conduct any urban exploring in Dublin, as well as climbing or trekking in the parks. A must-have for any vacation, but particularly in touristic destinations like Dublin. Have a soft copy of your travel insurance on hand, and transmit your policy information to your main emergency contact.

- Credit and ATM cards (if your bank requires it, phone them to let them know you're going). Have either a soft copy or a couple of physical copies on hand. Never travel with just one card or account access. I keep two bank accounts and four credit cards. This way, if problems happen on the road (which they do), I'm not stranded. You never know when your credit card issuer may detect a foreign ATM withdrawal as suspicious and ban your cards.

What to Bring When Staying at Hostels

- Are you thinking about staying in a hostel? I've been in a few hostels in Ireland, and these are the essentials for a good, clean, and generally peaceful hostel stay:
- Flip-flops or shower shoes: I mentioned this before, but it's especially crucial if you're staying in a hostel and want to keep your feet covered in the shower.

- Full-Sized Travel Towel: This is the greatest travel towel in the world, and you'll need it if you stay in hostels that require you to carry your own towel.
- A lock: Most hostels need this for your locker.
- Bring Your Own Privacy: If you're a light sleeper, bring a Sleep Mask and Earplugs to shut out the other hostel guests.

What to Bring to Study Abroad, Work Abroad, and Homestays

If you are staying with someone or dealing with anybody in Ireland who may be regarded as "hosting you," it is customary to bring a modest gift from home to offer to your hosts. Popular options for this sort of present include products that are only available in your home country, like anything with your home nation's flag on it or something created there. This does not have to be lavish; a tiny gesture would suffice.

Chapter 4

Northern Ireland's Best Beaches and Islands

Northern Ireland's greatest beaches are surrounded by charming conservation communities, Areas of Outstanding Natural Beauty, and historic sand dune systems.

Wildlife enthusiasts may keep an eye out for unique flora and marine critters like puffins, dolphins, and even orcas. Families may relax on award-winning sandy stretches as surfers hit the waves. If you like history, you will enjoy touring castle ruins and medieval religious structures.

Whether you want to learn about the local culture, admire some of the greatest natural vistas in the UK, or participate in water activities ranging from jet skiing to kite surfing, Northern Ireland has a beach for you.

1. Beach on West Strand

Best for: • Families • Photography • Budget • Adventure

West Strand Beach is located near the coastal town of Portrush and is bounded to the north by a port and to the east by a promenade. This beach, which is home to several of Northern Ireland's oldest surf schools, becomes one of the UK's most popular surfing locations throughout the summer. Outside of the summer, popular activities include dog walking, horseback riding, and traversing coastal paths.

If you're an experienced surfer, go to West Strand Beach in the winter for the finest waves, but remember to wear a full-body swimsuit to protect yourself from the chilly water. July and August are ideal months to come with the family since all of the adjacent amusements and arcades are open, and experienced lifeguards increase safety for swimmers and surfers of all skill levels.

- **Address**: West Strand Beach, W Strand Rd, Portrush BT56 8ET, United Kingdom

2. Beach at Ballintoy Harbour

Best for: • Photography • Budget • Couples • History • Adventure

Ballintoy Harbour Beach is distinguished by its craggy rock walls and magnificent ocean scenery. The little hilly islands right off the shore were portrayed as the Iron Islands in the blockbuster television series Game of Thrones. While admiring the natural beauty of Ballintoy Harbour, keep an eye out for colorful butterflies, seabirds, and, if you're fortunate, dolphins.

After spending the day at this peaceful beach, visit the surrounding town of Ballintoy, which offers stores, cafés, restaurants, and sights like the Ballintoy Church, which has a distinct Latin aspect. If you wish to view more natural marvels, drive around 15 minutes from Ballintoy to the UNESCO-protected Giant's Causeway, a creation of about 40,000 basalt rocks.

- **Address**: Harbour Rd, Ballintoy, Ballycastle BT54 6NA, United Kingdom

3. Beach Benone

Best for: • Families • Photography • Budget • Adventure

Benone Beach is one of Northern Ireland's longest beaches, covering around 7 miles of golden sand. Windy weather conditions make this beach popular for kiting and watersports, but its clear, rock-free waters provide for a relaxing swim, particularly during the summer and on public holidays.

Nature enthusiasts often traverse the surrounding protected sand dunes' boardwalks. Keep an eye out for animals, including birds, seals, and porpoises. On a clear day, you can see the Binevenagh Mountain, the breathtaking beauty of Donegal, and the Scottish shore. For the youngsters, there is also a supervised playground and an outdoor paddle pool.

- **Address**: Benone Beach, Benone Ave, Limavady, United Kingdom

4. Beach at Castlerock

Best for: • Families • Photography • Budget • Couples • History • Adventure

Castlerock Beach, which is bounded to the east by the Lower River Bann estuary and to the west by the Downhill cliffs, is popular with families, water sports enthusiasts, and nature lovers alike. Castlerock Beach has been declared an Area of Outstanding Natural Beauty and an Area of Special Scientific Interest due to its spectacular landscape, ancient dunes, and wildlife reserves.

Don't miss the clifftop Mussenden Temple and neighboring Downhill Castle. These 18th-century buildings provide panoramic views of Castlerock and its surrounding natural beauties. Head into the village to discover restaurants, shops, and Hazlett House, a 17th-century thatched home that is said to be Northern Ireland's oldest.

- **Address**: Castlerock Beach, 4 Sea Rd, Castlerock, Coleraine BT51 4RE, United Kingdom

5. Downhill Beach

Best for: • Photography • Budget • Couples

Downhill Beach is set between sand dunes, flowing waterfalls, and stunning cliffs in the Bineveagh Area of Outstanding Natural Beauty. Water sports like jet skiing, canoeing, and kite surfing are popular at this Blue Flag beach, but its 7-mile expanse of sand and gentle waves make it perfect for paddling, sunbathing, and fishing.

Visit the Ulster Wildlife Trust Nature Reserve to witness birds, insects, and unique plant species that dwell in the undisturbed dune system, or go down to the beach early to see the dawn over the Mussenden Temple. Watch trains speed out of the Tunnel Brae, which runs through the rocks to the east of the shore. Parking is allowed on the beach all year.

- **Address:** Downhill Strand, Coleraine, United Kingdom

6. Island of Rathlin

Best for: • Photography • Budget • Couples

Rathlin Island, the northernmost point of Northern Ireland, offers panoramic views of the Causeway Coast on the mainland. This SAC is well-known for its big bird colony, which includes puffins that travel here from April to July. Rathlin Island's natural beauty is typified by spectacular cliffs, some of which rise as high as 230 feet.

Hike the paths and bridges that extend between the cliffs for a day of adventure, or traverse the coastline along Mill Bay to observe seals and seagulls. Learn about the island's historic shipwrecks and rich history at the Boathouse Visitor Centre. The island is just 6 miles distant and can be reached by boat from Ballycastle Boat Terminal.

- **Address:** Rathlin Island, Ballycastle, UK

7. Beach Whiterocks

Best for: • Families • Photography • Budget • Adventure

Whiterocks Beach, also known as The White Rocks, is notable for its spectacular white limestone cliffs and the labyrinth of arches and tunnels etched into them over millennia. Its powerful waves attract surfers and bodyboarders, but sunbathers will enjoy the beauty and cleanliness of the 3-mile-long Blue Flag beach.

Whiterocks Beach has a lifeguard service, making it an ideal family beach location. Horseback riding and dog walking are prohibited in July and August, but these are the finest months to learn to surf at neighboring schools like Troggs Surf School. Portrush, the nearest town, has restaurants, stores, and entertainment places like Barry's Amusements.

- **Address**: Portrush Whiterocks Beach, Portrush BT56 8DF, United Kingdom

8. National Nature Reserve Murlough

Best for: • Families • Photography • Budget • Couples • History • Adventure

The Murlough National Nature Reserve, located on the coast of County Down, contains a 6,000-year-old dune system, a shingle beach, and a 4-mile Blue Flag sandy length with outstanding views of the Mourne Mountains and Dundrum Bay. In addition to being a popular trekking destination, the reserve is a wildlife-viewing paradise. You could encounter seals, porpoises, dolphins, or even orcas if you're fortunate.

Visit the adjacent conservation community of Strangford to visit the port, Northern Ireland's first marine nature reserve, and the Area of Outstanding Natural Beauty Strangford Lough. Take the boat over the lough to Portaferry, where you may enjoy the ancient gardens of the 16th-century Portaferry Castle.
- **Address**: Dundrum, Newcastle BT33 0NQ, United Kingdom

9. Tyrella Bay

Best for: • Families • Photography • Budget • History • **Adventure**

Tyrella Beach is a mile-long sandy beach backed by the Mourne Mountains and around 25 acres of sand dunes that create the Dundrum Bay conservation area. During the summer, families, surfers, and water sports enthusiasts flock to the car-free beach. The dunes attract wildlife enthusiasts looking for unique flora and creatures all year.

Tyrella Beach is approximately 5 miles from Clough, where you can see the remnants of a 12th-century Anglo-Norman castle perched on a 25-foot-high motte. About 3 miles from Clough lies the charming hamlet of Dundrum, which has a variety of restaurants and stores. Visit Dundrum Bay after sunset for spectacular views.

- **Address**: Tyrella Beach, Downpatrick BT30 8SU, United Kingdom

10. Cushendun Beach

Best for: • Families • Photography • Budget • Couples • Adventure

On a clear day, Cushendun Beach is tucked in a cove by the lovely settlement of Cushendun and offers views across the magnificent Mull of Kintyre. It draws history aficionados who want to see the 14th-century Carra Castle Ruins and neighboring Bronze-Age standing stones. If you like fantasy, visit the stunning Red Caves, which served as a shooting site for Game of Thrones.

Water sports, sunbathing, and touring are popular pastimes. However, be warned that there is no lifeguard service and that dog walking restrictions apply throughout the summer. When you're feeling peckish, stop into The Corner House, a classic tearoom preserved by the National Trust.

- **Address**: 4 Maud Cottages, Cushendun, Ballymena BT44 0PJ, United Kingdom

Best Things To Do

There is so much to do in Northern Ireland, yet many people never go beyond Belfast and the Causeway Coast, which is unfortunate since many of the nicest spots to visit in Northern Ireland are seldom included on the covers of glossy tourist guidebooks!

In this guide, we've included both off-the-beaten-path hidden treasures (like Torr Head) and popular tourist destinations in Northern Ireland (like the Antrim Glens). Dive right in!

The Top Activities in Northern Ireland

Northern Ireland's six counties (Antrim, Armagh, Down, Derry, Tyrone, and Fermanagh) are an explorer's dream - here are our top picks!

1. Coastal Route of the Causeway

The Causeway Coastal Route connects Belfast and Derry and is 120 miles long. It's a breathtaking trip that takes you past several of Northern Ireland's top attractions.

Although it is possible to drive everything in a single day, we suggest allowing at least two to three days to soak in the scenery, stroll about some beautiful towns, and do some of the different treks and walks.

Along the road, popular attractions include the Giant's Causeway, Dunluce Castle, and the Carrick-a-rede rope bridge, among many more.

- **Address:** Causeway Coastal Route, Ballintoy, Ballycastle BT54 6NE, United Kingdom

2. Forest Park of Tollymore

Tollymore Forest Park is located near the Mourne Mountains. It covers approximately 1,500 acres and offers breathtaking views of the surrounding mountains and the Irish Sea.

With four well-marked pathways and various intriguing structures and historical elements, the park is jam-packed with things to do and see.

Choose the Blue Arboretum Path, a 0.8km route that winds through one of Ireland's oldest arboretums (a botanical park dedicated to trees).

Visit the Barbican Gate, as well as the magnificent Stone Bridges and the magical Hermitage. For good reason, this is one of the top spots to visit in Northern Ireland!

- **Address**: Bryansford Rd, Newcastle BT33 0PR, United Kingdom

3. The majestic Mourne Mountains

The Mourne Mountains are Northern Ireland's most spectacular mountain range, and they are home to the country's highest peak, Slieve Donard, which stands at 850 meters.

C.S. was inspired by the range's raw beauty and dramatic sceneries. Lewis's Chronicles of Narnia is a walker's dream!

From Slieve Doan and Slieve Binnian to the enormous Slieve Bearnagh, there's a variety of pathways to choose from. The length and complexity of the paths vary.

If you want to do something physical in Northern Ireland, you could easily spend a weekend in Newcastle and complete many of the hikes over the course of a few days.

- **Address**: Newry BT34 5XL, UK

4. Black Cab Tours in Belfast

If you're looking for something to do in Northern Ireland that will offer you a decent insight into the country's volatile history, go no further than the Belfast Black Cab Tours.

This is a very unique way to experience the city and is a must-do for anybody visiting Belfast! It's no secret that Belfast has had a stormy history, and Black Cab Tours (provided by long-term locals) can provide you with an in-depth insight into what it was like to live in the city during those times.

There are various firms that provide Black Cab trips, and depending on the one you choose, they may offer somewhat different tours/routes.

The excursions take you past the Belfast murals, down the Falls Road and the Shankill Road, and past many of the city's most renowned attractions.

5. There are castles everywhere.

There are several castles in Northern Ireland for individuals who want to go back in time.

Dunluce Castle, Belfast Castle, Kinbane Castle, Carrickfergus Castle, Castle Ward, and Dunseverick Castle are some of the more noteworthy castles.

Carrickfergus Castle is perhaps Northern Ireland's most well-known castle. The castle, which dates back to 1177, is in perfect shape and has a postcard-worthy setting directly on the ocean.

Belfast Castle is a must-see if you're seeking a castle suited for a Disney Princess. It's one of the most attractive castles in Ireland, with stunning towers and wonderful gardens!

6. Torr Head Scenic Drive

The Torr Head Scenic Route (a small diversion off the Causeway Coast) is one of the most unusual things to do in Northern Ireland.

With 23km of tight roads, bendy curves, and countless blind spots, the trip between Cushendun and Ballycastle is not for the faint of heart.

If you are ready for the struggle, you will be rewarded with breathtaking views. Scotland may be seen in the distance on a clear day!

It takes around 40 minutes from start to finish without breaks, although we suggest taking a few diversions to view Murlough Bay, the Fair Head Cliffs, and, of course, Torr Head.

7. The Causeway of the Giants

The Giant's Causeway is one of Northern Ireland's most famous tourist attractions, and although it's definitely worth a visit, enormous crowds, expensive parking, and terrible weather may make or break your trip.

The Giant's Causeway is a UNESCO World Heritage monument that was constructed by volcanic activity between 50 and 60 million years ago.

However, according to tradition, the gigantic Causeway was created by gigantic Fionn mac Cumhaill in order for him to cross the Irish Sea and combat Benandonner, a Scottish giant!

A 10-minute walk from the property, we suggest parking at the Causeway Coast Way Car Park. It costs £10 per vehicle. However, it is far less expensive than purchasing "Visitor Experience" tickets, which include parking at the tourist center.

- **Address**: Bushmills BT57 8SU, United Kingdom

8. The Kodak Corner

Another popular activity in Northern Ireland is a morning hike up to Kodak Corner. This is a beautiful place with stunning views of Carlingford Lough in Kilbroney Forest Park in Down.

The Cloughmore Trail is a nice 4.1km looping hike that leads to the viewpoint via Fiddler's Green.

Begin the hike at the top car park at Kilbroney. Follow the path to the "Big Stone," which, according to Irish legend, was hurled from across the lough by the giant Fionn mac Cumhail.

Following the stone, take a diversion down the dip to the left of the stone and continue the route to Kodak Corner! After that, you may either return to the stone and complete the circle or go back to the car park.

9. Forest Park of Glenariff

Glenariff Forest Park has 247 acres of forest, lakes, and waterfalls. With various gorgeous routes available, it's a perfect place for a quick stroll or a longer walk.

With a tea shop, picnic area, and BBQ facilities, the park is ideal for a party or family outing. The 3km waterfall hike is a necessity for first-time visitors.

Try the 1km Viewpoint Trail, which winds through the gorgeous gardens and provides beautiful views.

A visit here during the off-season, when crowds are lower, is one of the finest things to do in Northern Ireland, in our view, since there's a surprise around every turn.

Address: Glenariff Forest, Ballymena, UK

10. The shooting sites for Game of Thrones

Northern Ireland was heavily utilized in the production of HBO's Game of Thrones, with a total of 25 sites used! The Dark Hedges, utilized for the route from King's Landing, is one of the most recognizable locales.

If you're a die-hard fan of Game of Thrones, you may be more interested in Castle Ward, which was used to shoot Winterfell, and Tollymore Forest Park, which was used to film the Wolfswood near Winterfell, the Haunted Forest North of the Wall, and more.

The Game of Thrones Studio just opened in Banbridge, but if you want to explore the natural surroundings, check out our guide to the numerous Game of Thrones shooting sites throughout Ireland.

11. Crumlin Road Prison

The Crumlin Road Gaol, located near Belfast, was built in 1846. Before its closure in 1996, it was a fully operational prison for 150 years. The jail housed a diverse mix of detainees, including suffragettes, republicans, and loyalists.

The jail is not only available for visits, but it is also a performance venue and home to the Cuffs Bar & Grill, a licensed restaurant.

Take a self-guided tour (typically 60-90 minutes) or a fully guided tour (90 minutes) to get a true understanding.

The tunnel from the goal to the courtroom, the holding cells, and the eerie Hangman's Cell are among the attractions. This is a wonderful shout if you're wondering what to do in Northern Ireland while it's pouring.

12. The Scenic Drive to Slieve Gullion

The Slieve Gullion Scenic journey is a beautiful 10-kilometer journey via winding mountain roads and woodland. Begin from the Slieve Gullion Lower Car Park and return along the one-way tarmacked road around the mountain's southern and western borders.

There is a parking area at the top of the road where you may enjoy the views and have a picnic or trek to the summit of Slieve Gullion (the highest peak in County Armagh at 576 meters). The Peak has two Bronze Age cairns and breathtaking vistas. It's 1.5 kilometers back and forth from the higher parking lot.

If you're searching for the greatest things to do in Northern Ireland while it's raining, this is another wonderful choice since you can enjoy the scenery from the comfort of your vehicle.

13. Cuilcagh (the Irish Stairway to Heaven)

The Cuilcagh Boardwalk Trail (also known as Ireland's Stairway to Heaven) is an 11-kilometer trek across Northern Ireland's biggest section of blanket bog in County Fermanagh.

You may park at the Cuilcagh Boardwalk car park (£6 and must be reserved in advance) near the trail's entrance or in the Killykeegan Nature Reserve car park (free) 1km further on.

The trek is quite difficult, taking most people between two and three hours to accomplish, but you'll be rewarded with breathtaking views of the swamp and the boardwalk disappearing into the distance!

Because this is one of Northern Ireland's most popular physical activities, it may become extremely crowded on weekends!

- **Address**: Marble Arch Road, Enniskillen BT92 1EW, United Kingdom

14. The Distillery at Old Bushmills

The Old Bushmills Distillery is the oldest legal whiskey distillery in the world. Few tourist sites in Northern Ireland generate as large crowds as this one!

It has been creating triple-distilled single malt whiskey using 100% malted barley for nearly 400 years. It's a lovely little excursion off the Causeway Coastal Route and a chance to explore a functioning distillery!

Tours last around an hour and include the opportunity to learn about the distillation process as well as view the copper stills, barrels, and casks. The tour concludes at the 1608 bar, where you may sample one of Ireland's most famous whiskey brands.

- **Address**: 2 Distillery Rd, Bushmills BT57 8XH, United Kingdom

15. The Sperrin family

The Sperrins are one of Northern Ireland's most ignored tourist attractions, yet they are definitely worth considering during your visit.

The Sperrins are a declared Area of Outstanding Natural Beauty and one of the country's greatest highland regions, located on the border of counties Tyrone and Derry.

The Beaghmore Stone Circles, a circle of seven Bronze Age stones, may be found southeast of the Sperrin Mountain range.

Visit the Dark Sky Observatory in Davagh Forest for an unforgettable experience. It is ideal for astronomy because of the absence of light pollution, and there is an outdoor viewing platform.

16. The Cave Hill trek

One of our favorite things to do in Belfast is the Cave Hill climb. The journey takes you through Cave Hill Country Park and is difficult for the faint of heart.

A tough 7.2km loop. Most people start at Belfast Castle and follow the green arrows.

Begin by ascending the route from the parking lot, then turn right and continue into the forest. Ascend through the woods to the plateau for spectacular views of Belfast!

McArt's Fort, the Devil's Punchbowl, and, of course, more breathtaking vistas are highlights along the journey.

- **Address:** Cavehill, Newtownabbey BT36 7WH, United Kingdom

17. The Belfast Titanic

Titanic Belfast, with nine interactive exhibits, is the world's largest Titanic tourist experience. The self-guided Titanic Experience and the guided Discovery Tour are also offered.

You may explore the galleries like the Shipyard Ride, The Maiden Voyage, and The Sinking during the Titanic Experience.

It also covers passage on the SS Nomadic, the ship that transported first and second-class passengers from Cherbourg to the Titanic.

The Discovery Tour is a one-hour outdoor stroll led by a tour guide wearing a roaming headset. During the tour, you'll learn about the ship's construction, its last hours, and the "easter eggs" hidden throughout the Titanic Belfast structure.

- **Address**: 1 Olympic Way, Belfast BT3 9EP, United Kingdom

18. Marble Arch Caverns

The Marble Arch caverns are a collection of limestone caverns and subterranean waterways located in the Cuilcagh Mountain foothills. Although just 1.5km of the cave and river system is viewable during excursions, it stretches 11km beneath.

The caverns are the ultimate underground experience, with a 60-minute guided tour available. On the Owenbrean River - Walking Cave Tour, you'll see pools and secret tunnels, as well as follow the river as it carves a course through the stone.

Those who attend while the subsurface water levels are sufficiently high will be automatically upgraded to the Martel Tour (an additional 15 minutes), which includes a small boat ride!

If you're wondering what to do in Northern Ireland this weekend, start with the Cuilcagh climb and then go on to the caves!
Address: 43 Marlbank Rd, Enniskillen BT92 1EW, United Kingdom

19. Strand of Portstewart

The National Trust manages Portstewart Strand, a beautiful Blue Flag beach. The beaches' excellent golden sand and abundance of animals make it immensely popular, stretching for 3.2km.

The beach is surrounded by 6,000-year-old sand dunes that are home to native flora and butterflies, with some dunes reaching a height of 30 meters!

The Portstewart Strand - Sand Dune & Estuary Trail is a great way to get your legs moving, with magnificent coastal vistas along the way.

Portstewart Strand, located on the Causeway Coast, is another G.O.T. filming site and a lovely area for a swim, a surf, or a family picnic.

- **Address:** Portstewart Strand and Barmouth, Portstewart BT55 7AJ, United Kingdom

20. Rope Bridge at Carrick-a-rede

Few sites to visit in Northern Ireland are as well-documented as our next stop. The Carrick-a-Rede Rope Bridge was erected in 1755 by salmon fishermen to link Carrick-a-Rede to the mainland.

Fortunately, it has been renovated throughout the years, and it is now an exciting (but robust) 20-metre walkover, hung 30 metres above the lake!

Once reaching the island, stop to appreciate the lone white-washed home, a remnant of the island's fishing heritage, which ended in 2002.

- **Address**: Ballintoy, Antrim, Ballycastle, United Kingdom

21. The Peninsula of Ards

The Ards Peninsula in County Down is a beautiful part of Northern Ireland with unique sights and rolling green hills. Donaghadee, Newtownards, and Ballywalter are among the towns and villages on the peninsula.

Strangford Lough, the biggest marine lough in the United Kingdom, is bordered by the peninsula. The lough is excellent for birding since it attracts three-quarters of the world's Brent Geese population throughout the winter.

Scrabo Tower at Newtownards, Grey Monastery, a 12th-century Cistercian monastery ruin, and Portaferry, a picturesque port community, are all must-sees on the Ards Peninsula.

- **Address:** Ards Peninsula, Newtownards BT22 1BS, UK

22. Murlough Bay

Murlough Beach is a 6.4 km-long beach in County Down that is framed by the majestic Mourne Mountains. The National Trust manages the Blue Flag beach, which has a summer lifeguard service and on-site parking, albeit it is a short walk across the dunes.

Murlough Nature Reserve's vast dune structure behind the shore stretches back 6,000 years! It is home to a wide variety of animals and plants and was established as Ireland's first nature reserve in 1967.

If you're searching for exciting things to do in Northern Ireland this weekend, trek Slieve Donard first, then grab some dinner in Newcastle before going for a sand ramble!

23. St. Patrick's Cathedral (or Cathedrals)

In Armagh, there are two St. Patrick's Cathedrals, one for the Roman Catholic Church and the other for the Church of Ireland. Both are finely constructed and although they are not interchangeable, they are related.

St. Patrick's Cathedral (Church of Ireland) is on the site of a stone monastery constructed by St. Patrick in the fifth century.

The church was an important part of the Catholic Church of Ireland until it was taken over by the Church of Ireland during the Irish Reformation in the 16th century.

This resulted in the establishment of the other St. Patrick's (Roman Catholic), which was constructed between 1840 and 1904, a historically and politically significant undertaking.

24. The Divis Peak Trail

The Divis Summit Trail is a 4.5-kilometer circle trek that traverses Divis Mountain. It offers breathtaking views of Belfast, Lough Neagh, and the Irish Sea.

It's a modest hike up to the 478-meter top, where you can take in panoramic views of the city and beyond.

The red way-marked route begins at the top car park. However, a lower car park is a short walk away.

Both are administered by the National Trust and may be rather popular on sunny days.

25. Glen, Colin

Colin Glen is one of the most popular family activities in Belfast! This is a family-friendly adventure park located just outside of town!

It is home to the country's first Alpine Coaster, the country's longest zipline, and several more attractions. The 200-acre park is densely forested, has a river running through it, and even features a 9-hole golf course.

The Black Bull Run, a 565-metre roller coaster through the Colin Glen Forest, the Gruffalo & Stickman Guided Walk (excellent for small kids!), and the SKYTrek ropes course, a 50-foot-high course featuring a 90-metre zipline, are all must-do activities.

For good reason, Colin Glen is often considered one of the top things to do in Northern Ireland with kids.

Top Museums

The Northern Ireland Troubles lasted from 1968 to 1998, resulting in approximately 3,600 fatalities and many more injuries. Northern Ireland is now a peaceful nation. However, sharing the history of numerous historical events, not only The Troubles, is an essential aspect of Northern Irish culture.

We've included some of the greatest museums in the nation where you can see this fascinating history for yourself and learn more about Northern Ireland.

The Belfast Titanic

The Titanic is a world-famous, historic passenger ship that formerly had a deep link to Northern Ireland and still does today. On April 2, 1912, the Titanic set sail from Belfast's Harland & Wolff shipyard for Southampton.

The Titanic Museum debuted in 2012. It is a six-story structure with nine stunning galleries that recount the Titanic's narrative from origin to conclusion, providing fascinating insight into the ship's rich history. Visitors to the museum may truly experience the sights, sounds, and emotions of the ship and the water, giving the experience a completely authentic atmosphere.

The museum immediately became one of Belfast's most popular tourist attractions, and it is unquestionably a must-see. The trip lasts around two hours on average. There are many audio tour guides available to give you all of the information in each gallery you visit. Titanic Belfast sells tickets for children, adults, students, and families, with prices varying. You may choose the sort of tour you want, so there is something for everyone.

- **Address**: 1 Olympic Wy, Belfast BT3 9EP, United Kingdom
- Opens 10 am
- Phone: +44 28 9076 6386

Botanic Court, Ulster Museum, Belfast

The Ulster Museum is sometimes referred to as Northern Ireland's "treasure house" because of its collection of fascinating facets of Northern Irish culture, both past and present.

The Ulster Museum is conveniently located next to the famed Queen's University and the lovely Botanic Gardens, making it ideal for anybody visiting Belfast City. The museum is within walking distance of Botanic Avenue and Stranmillis, both of which include a range of cafés, restaurants, corner shops, and pubs popular with visitors.

A trip to the Ulster Museum is something that the whole family will appreciate. You may learn about Northern Ireland's history as well as explore art from local and international artists. The museum features lots of interactive zones to keep young children interested and involved, as well as a café and gift store where you can buy souvenirs to commemorate your visit. The Botanic Gardens are attached to the museum grounds, so if the weather permits, you may have a picnic in the beautiful surroundings.

One of the nicest parts about visiting this museum is that it is completely free. So you may bring the whole family and not have to pay an admission price. It's the ideal spot to take youngsters during the summer vacations or for adults to spend a leisurely day diving into history and art, particularly if you're on a budget.

- Address: Botanic Gardens, Belfast BT9 5AB, United Kingdom
- Opens 10 am
- Phone: +44 28 9044 0000

The Folk and Transport Museum

This is one of several museums owned by "National Museums Northern Ireland," which also owns the Ulster Museum. The Folk and Transport Museum highlights Northern Ireland's history, culture, and inventiveness, with structures and transportation spanning back 100 years.

This museum is divided into two sub-museums: the Transport Museum and the Folk Museum. You may take the whole museum tour, which includes both portions. However, bear in mind that you'll most likely need a whole day to really appreciate it. The Folk Museum is comprised of historic homes, stores, schools, and churches. There are live actors, which adds to the sense of being transported back in time. The majority of the buildings are available to the public, and although some are copies, many are originals.

The Irish Railway collection, Road Transport Galleries, and Land, Sea, and Sky Galleries are all on display in the Transport Museum. This museum's large transportation collection depicts how people moved to, from, and within Northern Ireland throughout the past century.
- Address: Cultra, Holywood BT18 0EU, United Kingdom
- Opened: 1967
- Closes 4 pm
- Phone: +44 28 9042 8428

The Ulster American Folk Park, Omagh, County Tyrone

The Ulster American Folk Park is an open-air museum in County Tyrone, Northern Ireland, located west of Omagh. The museum depicts the tale of three centuries of Irish emigration via more than 30 display structures.

The museum concentrates on individuals who left Ulster for America in the 18th, 19th, and 20th centuries, with costumed interpreters and exhibits of traditional crafts. The museum is a branch of the National Museums of Northern Ireland.

- Address: 2 Mellon Rd, Omagh BT78 5QU, United Kingdom
- Founded: 1976
- Closes 4 pm
- Phone: +44 28 8224 3292

Belfast's Linen Hall Library, Donegall Square

The Linen Hall Library is absolutely one-of-a-kind. It is the oldest library in Belfast and the only existing library in Ireland that derives a part of its revenue from membership.

The library is open to the public and is situated in a beautiful old Victorian linen warehouse on Donegall Square, opposite Belfast City Hall. It was founded on radical and "enlightenment" principles, and it has valued independence and the notion that its resources are held by the community for the community.

It is known for its unrivaled Irish and Local Studies Collection, which includes extensive holdings of Early Belfast and Ulster printed publications, as well as the 350,000-item Northern Ireland Political Collection, which is the authoritative record of the recent 'Troubles.'

- Address: 17 Donegall Square N, Belfast BT1 5GB, United Kingdom
- Closes 5:30 pm
- Phone: +44 28 9032 1707

Banbridge, Co Down, Game of Thrones Studio Tour.

A €48 million Game of Thrones studio tour is situated in Banbridge, County Down, and is inspired by the famed HBO series. The Game of Thrones Studio Tour is held in the massive Linen Mills Studios, situated off the Dublin to Belfast route, and was one of 26 sites in Northern Ireland utilized for filming over the eight seasons of the enormously popular HBO program.

The studio tour includes authentic costumes, props, and life-sized replicas of the characters from the blockbuster show, as well as tens of thousands of weapons from the show, such as swords, spears, shields, and a big scorpion crossbow. This spellbinding trip will take fans deep into the kingdom of Westeros and beyond.

- Address: The Boulevard, Cascum Rd, Banbridge BT32 4LF, United Kingdom
- Closes 6:30 pm
- Phone: +44 28 4046 4777

Chapter 5

Food and Drink in Northern Ireland

Despite sharing an island, the cuisine of the Republic of Ireland is very unique from that of Northern Ireland. To the north, there is obviously more of a British influence. When visiting Northern Ireland, these are just a handful of the must-try delicacies.

It was strange for us to go to Northern Ireland. We've been visiting Ireland for two decades and reside in the south, but the north was a blank slate. We were interested in learning about Northern Ireland cuisine and how it differed from Irish food in the south and food in the United Kingdom.

We began our journey in Belfast and traveled west to Derry. We stopped in a few beach towns along the route to take in the scenery and learn about small-town life. Most importantly, we ate and drank our way around the area and really enjoyed ourselves.

Northern Ireland Food

This section discusses special Northern Ireland cuisine that you must try while visiting this far north area. In this region of the globe, much like our Edinburgh Travel Guide, it's difficult to identify what's "Irish" and what's "British." To be honest, I have no idea what Northern Ireland's national dish is.

Having said that, our suggestions in this area are based on what we ate in Northern Ireland and the research we conducted before our trip. Most importantly, it stems from our years of dining in

Ireland, which prompted us to consider what makes eating in Northern Ireland special and different.

The Ulster Fry is a Northern Irish breakfast dish.

Our typical breakfast consists of fresh fruit, yogurt with muesli, and sometimes toast or a bagel. It is often a bowl of cereal. But when we arrive in Ireland, it means a nice fry, which is one of Ireland's most renowned features. During our time in Northern Ireland, we consumed an unusually high number of huge breakfast plates. Every hotel we stayed at offered a fry as a breakfast option.

The Ulster fry is a huge platter of morning delicacies that rapidly became one of my favorite Northern Irish cuisines. A fried egg with Irish pork sausage, rashers (a sort of bacon), black and white pudding, and typically beans or a grilled tomato half, served with bread and butter.

If you've never had black pudding, don't be frightened to try it. It's a tasty blood pudding shaped like a sausage made with pork, onions, oats, and pig blood. It's less horrifying than morcilla, the Spanish blood sausage, since it's more oatmeal than blood! Give it a go. If you're still doubtful, try the white pudding, which has comparable components but no blood.

Potato Bread with Soda Farl

Unlike the fries we're accustomed to in the South, the Northern Ireland version had two fried things we'd never tried before. The first was a fried slice of bread that went well with the liquid egg yolk.

The second was cooked and soft, similar to a potato but not as crispy as a hash brown. We did, however, get frequent toast. This meant that each Irish fry came with toast, fried bread, and fried potato.

After doing some research on bread, I discovered that fried bread is known as a soda farl. Soda farl is a soda bread or potato bread that is often eaten with fried. Whatever they name it, I adored this classic Northern Irish dish.

Baps are traditional Irish sandwich dishes.

We've been visiting Ireland for over two decades. I don't remember seeing any baps on any of those excursions. Burger buns are comparable to baps. They are stuffed with various components to form a sandwich.

Baps come in a variety of forms and sizes. The components for the morning bap are the same as for an Ulster Fry but in sandwich shape. Alternatively, try a bap with back bacon, a cured pig belly, and a drizzle of HP brown sauce. Yum!

Irish Boxty's

The Irish Potato Boxty is known by several different names. "Poundy," "Poundies," or its Gaelic names, "Bacstai" or "Aran bocht-ti," imply "poor-house bread". Whatever you name it, the Irish Potato Boxty is a basic and straightforward meal made of finely shredded potatoes, flour, baking soda, buttermilk, and sometimes eggs.

The outcome is a thick, rudely sliced pancake fried in butter. Boxties are often accompanied by a variety of side dishes such as salmon, rashers (bacon), black or white puddings, or fried eggs. This dish is linked with County Mayo in both the Republic of Ireland and Ulster.

Salmon from Ireland

We like fish but have never liked salmon. Something about it simply doesn't appeal to us as much as other varieties of fish. This is sad since native Irish salmon may be found in practically every dish.

In Ireland, salmon is a natural fish species. Salmon may be found prospering in several freshwater rivers across the North and South. Salmon, which is high in omega-3 fatty acids, is frequently smoked in Ireland. Smoking salmon helps preserve it prior to refrigeration. Salmon is available chilled, grilled, or in a steaming bowl of seafood chowder. Smoked salmon is another popular beginning.

Local Seafood And Lobster

It should come as no surprise that Ireland has fantastic seafood. After all, it is an island. Northern Ireland benefits from a diverse range of seafood due to the frigid waters of the North Atlantic Ocean. For many years, the majority of the seafood harvested off the coast of Ireland was exported. Fortunately, that tendency is changing.

Scallops, mussels, and oysters fished locally may be found in restaurants around Northern Ireland. There are even lobsters and crabs. Cod, skate, and turbot, among many other fish species, live in the seas around Northern Ireland.

Dillisk, seaweed, or dulse

This is not something for the faint of heart. Northern Ireland's shore has a historical history of foraging for seaweed. Various species of seaweed are used in both modern and traditional Northern Irish dishes. Soups, main courses, and desserts are all available. Dulse, a dried, salty seaweed nibble, is a traditional Northern Irish cuisine. It makes a good beer snack, although it is an acquired taste.

Scones

Scones are one of the most typically Irish or English foods, depending on who you ask. Scones are said to have originated in Scotland in the 16th century. Regardless of who or when scones originated, let us celebrate that they are widely available across Northern Ireland.

Scones are best served with afternoon tea and may be prepared with wheat or oats. To lighten the mixture, baking powder is used as a leavening agent. They are just exquisite when baked and served with cream & jam. Our hotel, the Beech Hill Country Hotel, had the nicest scones we had in Northern Ireland.

Victoria's Secret

The Victoria Sponge Cake, named after Queen Victoria, is a famous dish in Derry (Londonderry). So remarked our tour guide. The cake dates back to the mid-nineteenth century, during

Queen Victoria's reign. At the time, the Victoria Sponge was exclusively served with jam. The addition of cream gives this delectable dish a contemporary edge.

The cake is rich and delicious on its own. Making it quite filling. If you're feeling really gluttonous, an extra pot of cream is provided on the side. The Victoria Sponge Cake may be found in pastry shops and on dessert menus across Northern Ireland.

Pudding with Bread and Butter

With a few exceptions, we are not dessert people in general. One such exception is bread and butter pudding. In the United States, it's known as bread pudding, and it's a perfect example of not wasting food. Stale or day-old bread is used in bread and butter pudding.

Bread and butter pudding is produced by stacking buttered bread pieces in a pan with egg and cream, maybe raisins and cinnamon. It is soft, gooey, and heavenly when it comes out of the oven. The bread and butter pudding we had at Beech Hill Hotel's Ardmore Restaurant was definitely a piece of culinary genius.

Pudding with Sticky Toffee

Sticky toffee pudding is another fantastic British-style dessert. It's a huge, delicious sponge cake topped with toffee sauce. Unfortunately, some versions may be overly sweet. Other variants are topped with fresh vanilla ice cream, practically a la mode.

Our sticky toffee pudding at Harry's Shack in Portstewart was well-balanced and not too sugary. The views of the river enhanced the flavor of the pudding.

Northern Irish Candies

Northern Ireland excels at a few confections. Some of them may appear on an Irish food list, while others may seem more British, but they are all worth a try.

Caramel squares, which are bits of Irish shortbread covered with caramel and fudge, are a good option. What could possibly go wrong? Jammy Joeys is another traditional Irish dish from the north. It's a delicious sponge cake with jam and coconut on top. They are available at bakeries as well as convenience shops.

Northern Ireland enjoys beer and cider.

There's no lack of Guinness to be had in Northern Ireland, but there are other possibilities. Tennents from Scotland is a pleasant beer to look for. There are also a few English cask ales on tap. Cask ales are quite popular in the United Kingdom. However, they are an acquired taste. They vary from other beers in that they are unfiltered and unpasteurized, giving them a unique flavor.

Northern Ireland Craft Beer

Craft beer, often known as independent beer brewing, has grown in popularity in both the Republic of Ireland and Northern Ireland during the last decade. A number of craft beer breweries have sprouted from Belfast to Derry. Craft beer in Northern Ireland, like other craft beer manufacturers across the globe, is regional. That is, many breweries do not transport their beers outside of Ireland or the United Kingdom. So make use of them while you can.

Walled City Brewery in Derry, Lacada in Portrush, and Hilden Brewery in Lisburn (10 miles outside of Belfast) are a few names to watch out for. The Hilden Brewery has the distinction of being Ireland's first microbrewery. It opened its doors for the first time in 1981.

If you can't visit these brewers in person, come to Sunflower in Belfast's center to enjoy their extensive selection of independent beers. They serve both Irish and international craft beers in their outdoor beer garden.

If you're tired of stouts, porters, and IPAs, look for locally-made ciders. Northern Ireland, particularly County Armagh, has a long history of manufacturing high-quality ciders. They are a light and pleasant alternative to beer.

Gin and Whiskey

Northern Ireland is home to Bushmills Whiskey, one of the world's most well-known Irish whiskeys. The distillery is accessible for tours and tastings in the village of Bushmills. A short distance from the shore, a visit to the distillery may easily be combined with a visit to the famed Giants Causeway.

Along with Bushmills, look for the Echlinville and Rademon Estate distilleries. Each is available for public tours and tastings.

Whiskey may be the king of spirits in Northern Ireland, but gin has grown in popularity over the last decade. If you have the opportunity, try a couple of Northern Ireland gins. Gin brands to search for include Shortcross, Jawbox, and Boatyard.

Shopping in Northern Ireland

Northern Ireland recognizes the pleasure that a good day of shopping can provide. So, wherever you go, you'll discover first-rate shopping malls, fantastic local markets, boutique design stores, and artisan craft stores. All of these sites are ideal for picking up something unique as a present to bring home - or as a way to indulge yourself.

Belfast's Victoria Square Shopping Centre

Victoria Square is home to over 70 attractive stores and restaurants, including famous brands such as Ted Baker, Hollister, Tommy Hilfiger, LK Bennet, and Hugo Boss, to mention a few.

Head to the Dome for panoramic views of the city. You'll be able to view all the way to the iconic Harland & Wolff Cranes, also known as Samson and Goliath to the locals.

- Address: 1 Victoria Square, Belfast BT1 4QG, United Kingdom
- Closes 6 pm
- Opening date: 6 March 2008; 15 years ago
- Number of stores and services: 98
- Phone: +44 28 9032 2277

Belfast's CastleCourt Shopping Centre

The slogan of CastleCourt is simple: Shop. Eat. Play. Repeat. You can do this at over 80 high-street retailers, like Matalan, Vila, Dorothy Perkins, Miss Selfridge, New Look, and more.

- Address: Royal Ave, Belfast BT1 1DD, United Kingdom
- Closes 6 pm
- Opened: 1990
- Owner: Wirefox Castle Property Limited
- Number of stores and services: 77
- Phone: +44 28 9023 4591

Belfast's St. George's Market

One of Belfast's oldest and most colorful attractions is St. George's Market. All under one roof, you'll discover the finest of local products as well as specialty cuisine from across the globe. Look for fresh fruits and vegetables, artisan meats, and the greatest selection of seafood in Ireland - at the latest count, there were 23 fish booths alone.

Check out the soda farls, 'Belfast Baps,' Suki Tea, and Broughgammon goat's flesh for some added local flavor.

There are also antique and antique booths, clothing, and local craft vendors, as well as live music from local musicians.
- Address: 12 East Bridge St, Belfast BT1 3NQ, United Kingdom
- Opens 8 am Fri
- Phone: +44 28 9043 5704

Bloomfield Avenue in East Belfast.

Bloomfield Avenue's cool stores have a more distinct style. It's a shopper's paradise, and you're certain to find something exceptional. Siren, Peels Fashion Store, Harlequin, Annabelle Ladies Fashions, and Arabesque Shoe Shop (which has a terrific assortment of Italian and Spanish shoes and purses) are all excellent locations to begin your search.

County Antrim's Abbeycentre Shopping Centre

The Abbey Centre and its adjoining Valley Retail Park are popular among communities on the outskirts of Belfast. Next, Dunnes, Marks and Spencer, TK Maxx, B&M, and Matalan have all established themselves here. Synge and Byrne have made it the ideal destination for an excellent coffee and shopping stop.
- Address: Longwood Rd, Newtownabbey BT37 9UH, United Kingdom

- Hours:
- Open · Closes 9 pm
- Phone: +44 28 9086 8018

Ballymena in County Antrim.

Ballymena boasts a diverse mix of small businesses and department retailers. For fashion, try Primrose on Greenvale Street or larger boutiques like McKillens on Church Street and Camerons on Broughshane Street.

Nearby, Marmalade, and Pretty Woman are excellent for well-known and emerging designer apparel. And, with its Next Clearance and M&S Outlet shops, Junction One, just off the M2, is a destination in its own right.

Derry-Londonderry Craft Village

It's difficult to think of a more appealing setting than Derry's wonderfully Dickensian Craft Village. A restored 18th-century street joins a 19th-century plaza here. As a consequence, the neighborhood is home to a variety of artisan enterprises, including 70 local craftspeople, restaurants, and coffee shops.

Fine art prints, jewelry, glass, silks, tweeds, and knitwear, coexist with delicate soaps and fragrant candles. Edel McBride, the Aran knitwear designer favored by both Hillary Clinton and Sarah Jessica Parker, is also present.

- **Address:** Craft Village, Shipquay St, Londonderry BT48 6AR, UK

Coleraine in County Londonderry.

You've come to the correct spot if you're looking for unusual and fascinating little boutiques. Daisy Mae store on Belhouse Lane will appeal to antique lovers.

This is a timeless appeal for a contemporary era, specializing in replicating classic styles in apparel, footwear, and accessories. While at the Diamond Centre, be sure to stop into Bishops Footwear and Ken Young for the finest menswear in Ireland.

The Causeway Speciality Market, a lively food and drink market in the town center, takes place on the second Saturday of every month.

County Londonderry, Magherafelt

Magherafelt is also a popular shopping destination. Spoilt Bella, Sarah-Jane, and The Queen Bee all carry curated collections from Europe's leading designers. The Fashion House on Market Street is well worth a visit, as is the Four Seasons Boutique on Queen Street for desirable footwear and purses.

County Tyrone's Linen Green

The Linen Green is a magnificent upscale retail town in Moygashel. Quality homewares and interior stores such as Anthologie, Bedeck, Gareth McFarland Design Yard, and Lavish. Along with these, there are fashion boutiques like The Lingerie Room, Storey, and Panache Shoe Company.

County Fermanagh's Buttermarket

The Buttermarket in Enniskillen is the place to go if you're seeking unique art and crafts. Formerly a dairy market in the nineteenth century, it is now the core of Fermanagh's burgeoning craft sector, offering everything from unique art, pottery, and ceramics to handcrafted jewelry, textiles, and picture framing. Rebecca's Café also serves creative handmade fare.

County Down Boulevard

The Boulevard in Banbridge is well-known among value-conscious shoppers. It's certainly worth the journey to save up to 70% off retail pricing at Gap, Jaeger, LK Bennett, M&S, and other businesses. It is located near the major A1 Dublin to Belfast route and now includes an Omniplex Cinema.

Newry Quays, County Down

The Quays retail mall is located directly on the border of the Newry Canal, thus the name. With easy access from the M1 highway between Dublin and Belfast, there is ample parking in and around the center, as well as a bus station close.

Where to begin with the stores? Start with some of the most well-known brands, such as Marks and Spencer, Sainsbury's, H&M, River Island, Superdry, Next, Sports Direct, and Ernst Jones. Sostrene Grene has traveled all the way from Denmark, and there are also the heady aromas of Lush cosmetics to sample.

There's also a Trespass apparel and equipment shop here if you're planning a vacation to Northern Ireland's wonderful outdoors. Skechers, Stat Sports, Peter Mark, Pure Gym, O'Neill's clothing, Belleek Living, Pandora, Houston's, and Claire's are also located in the Quays.

There are also a variety of food and beverage places to pick from, including Subway, Café Nero, Eddie Rockets, Starbucks, Bravo Liive Cuisine, Deli Lites, Ground, and Cunninghams.

Chapter 6

5 days Northern Ireland Itinerary
DAY 1

Morning.

Start your day with a delicious breakfast at Made in Belfast Cathedral Quarter in the heart of the city. Afterward, visit the Titanic Belfast to learn about the city's maritime history and the famous Titanic. Take a walk along the Belfast Peace Wall to understand the city's troubled past.

Afternoon.

For lunch, head to The Great Room Restaurant and enjoy a delightful meal. Afterward, explore the Belfast City Hall and admire its stunning architecture. Visit the Ulster Museum to discover the rich history and art of Northern Ireland.

Evening.

Enjoy a delicious dinner at Deanes EIPIC, known for its exquisite cuisine. End the day with a visit to the Belfast Empire Music Hall for live music and entertainment.

DAY 2

Morning.

Start your day with a hearty breakfast at Benedict Restaurant. Then, embark on a scenic drive along the Antrim Coast Road to Carrickfergus Castle. Explore the castle's rich history and enjoy the panoramic views.

Afternoon.

Head to the Old Bushmills Distillery for a guided tour and whiskey tasting. Afterward, visit the iconic Giant's Causeway and marvel at the unique rock formations. Take a walk along the Dunluce Castle and capture stunning photos.

Evening.

Enjoy a delicious dinner at Hill Street Brasserie in Belfast. For a unique experience, visit The Barking Dog Belfast for drinks in their dog-friendly beer garden.

DAY 3

Morning.

Start your day with a scenic hike along the Glenshane Pass and immerse yourself in the stunning landscapes. Afterward, enjoy a coffee and breakfast at BaoBun.

Afternoon.

Visit the enchanting Dark Hedges, known for its appearance in Game of Thrones. Take a thrilling walk across the Carrick-a-Rede Rope Bridge and admire the breathtaking coastal views.

Evening.

Indulge in a seafood dinner at Mourne Seafood Bar and savor the fresh flavors of the region.

DAY 4

Morning.

Start your day in Derry with a visit to the Derry Giants Causeway Luxury Day Trip for a guided tour of the Giant's Causeway and other nearby attractions. Enjoy a quick breakfast at Ginger Bistrobe before the tour.

Afternoon.

Explore the historic Derry Peace Bridge and take a walk along the Derry Walls for panoramic views of the city. Visit the Crumlin Road Gaol to learn about its fascinating history.

Evening.

Enjoy dinner at The Muddlers Club, known for its innovative cuisine. Afterward, head to The Dirty Onion for live music and a vibrant atmosphere.

DAY 5

Morning.

Start your last day in Belfast with a delicious breakfast at Holohans At The Barge, known for its cozy atmosphere. Visit the Titanic's Dock and pump house to learn more about the city's maritime heritage.

Afternoon.

Explore the Belfast Castle and its beautiful gardens. Enjoy a leisurely lunch at The Plough Inn before visiting the Shankill and Belfast Falls Road to gain insight into the city's history.

Evening.

End your trip with a memorable dinner at Ox, known for its Michelin-starred cuisine. Raise a glass to your Northern Ireland adventure at Coppi, a trendy bar in Belfast.

Conclusion

As the final page turns, a bittersweet feeling washes over you.

Northern Ireland has unfolded before you like a storybook, its landscapes whispering tales of ancient giants and whispering fairies, its cities throbbing with the rhythm of modern life and timeless music.

You've trekked through rugged mountains, danced in historic pubs, and marveled at intricate castles that stand as testaments to a turbulent past. You've tasted the warmth of local hospitality, savored the creamy richness of a good Ulster fry, and sipped whiskey smooth as the rolling hills.

But beyond the tangible sights and sounds, you've carried away something deeper: a connection to a land that defies easy categorization. You've glimpsed the resilient spirit of a people who have weathered storms and emerged stronger, their humor ever-present, their warmth like a peat fire against the chill. You've discovered a land where ancient myths brush shoulders with cutting-edge technology, where tradition and innovation weave a vibrant tapestry.

Leaving Northern Ireland isn't an ending. It's a beginning. It's the start of a story you'll carry within you, a tale you'll weave into your own tapestry of life. As you board your plane, a whisper of longing stirs, but alongside it, a feeling of anticipation. You know, with absolute certainty, that this isn't goodbye, but merely "slán agat," a see you again, whispered on the wind of a land that will forever hold a piece of your heart.

Now, go forth, armed with memories and newfound knowledge. Share your stories, sing the praises of the Emerald Isle, and inspire others to embark on their own Northern Irish adventure. The magic of this land lies not just in its rolling hills and bustling cities but in the spirit it ignites within those who dare to explore its depths.

So, dear traveler, let this book be your companion, your guide, your reminder to keep the spirit of Northern Ireland alive. Until we meet again beneath the whispering skies, go n-éirí go geal leat – may good luck follow you wherever you roam.

Reference

Hoffman, E. (2022, February 2). Food and Drinks Destination, LLC. Retrieved December 29, 2023, from Food And Drink Destinations website: https://fooddrinkdestinations.com/northern-irish-food-and-drink-guide/

Cooke, S. (2023, November). 6 of the best museums in Northern Ireland. Retrieved December 29, 2023, from IrishCentral.com website: https://www.irishcentral.com/travel/museums-northern-ireland.amp

O'Hara, K. (2023, July 12). 29 Best Things to Do in Northern Ireland in 2024. Retrieved December 29, 2023, from The Irish Road Trip website: https://www.theirishroadtrip.com/things-to-do-in-northern-ireland/

10 Best Beaches in Northern Ireland - Take a Break Away from Belfast on the Beaches of Northern Ireland - Go Guides. (2023). Retrieved December 29, 2023, from Hotels.com website: https://www.hotels.com/go/northern-ireland/best-beaches-northern-ireland

Getting Around Northern Ireland. (2020, June 25). Retrieved December 29, 2023, from Discover Northern Ireland website: https://discovernorthernireland.com/blog/read/2020/06/getting-around-northern-ireland-b89

Katie. (2023, June 20). Accommodation Guide – Northern Ireland. Retrieved December 29, 2023, from Northern Ireland Holidays Travel Guide & Tips website:

https://northernirelandholidays.co.uk/accommodation-guide-northern-ireland/

Davidson, A. (2022, August 18). 10 weird and wonderful places to stay in Northern Ireland. Retrieved December 29, 2023, from NorthernIrelandWorld website: https://www.northernirelandworld.com/lifestyle/staycation/10-weird-and-wonderful-places-to-stay-in-northern-ireland-3810754?page=3

Katie. (2023, March 20). Traveling to Northern Ireland – Things you need to know. Retrieved December 29, 2023, from Northern Ireland Holidays Travel Guide & Tips website: https://northernirelandholidays.co.uk/travelling-to-northern-ireland/#visa

Malou. (2022, May 10). Authentic Vacations. Retrieved December 29, 2023, from Authentic Vacations website: https://www.authenticvacations.com/authentic-travel-tips-northern-ireland

Allan and Fanfan. (2018, December 3). When is the Best Time to Visit Northern Ireland? Best Seasons? Retrieved December 29, 2023, from It's Sometimes Sunny in Bangor: Tourism and Travel in Northern Ireland website: https://bangorni.com/best-time-to-visit-northern-ireland/

Smith, G. (2022, April 6). 5 reasons why you should plan a visit to Northern Ireland. Retrieved December 29, 2023, from Real Word website: https://www.trafalgar.com/real-word/5-reasons-why-you-should-plan-a-visit-to-northern-ireland/

Northern Ireland. (2019). Retrieved December 29, 2023, from TheSchoolRun website: https://www.theschoolrun.com/homework-help/northern-ireland#:~:text=Northern%20Ireland%20is%20part%20of, populated%20country%20in%20the%20UK

Printed in Dunstable, United Kingdom